ALLAN MORRISON is a prolific author; his previous books include *Last Tram tae Auchenshuggle*! which combines three of his passions: humour, nostalgia and Glasgow. His media appearances include *The One Show, The Riverside Show, Out of Doors* and *Good Morning Scotland*.

He is involved in charity work and after-dinner speaking, and is a member of his local Rotary club. Allan enjoys hill-walking, sport and travel, and is a keen football supporter. He and his wife live in the west of Scotland, and he is the proud grandfather of four grandchildren.

Haud That Bus!

The humorous adventures of
Bus Pass Barbara and Bus Pass Molly

ALLAN MORRISON

with illustrations by
BOB DEWAR

Luath Press Limited
EDINBURGH
www.luath.co.uk

First Published 2018

ISBN: 978-1-912147-57-1

The paper used in this book is recyclable. It is made
from low chlorine pulps produced in a low energy,
low emissions manner from renewable forests.

Printed and bound by
Martins the Printers, Berwick upon Tweed

Typeset in Sabon and MetaPlus by 3btype.com

Contents

Author's Comments and Acknowledgements

In the process of researching this book, I discovered there are many 'Bus Pass Girls' and 'Bus Pass Boys' out there, who, most days, use their free travel pass to advantage to enjoy trips throughout Scotland.

I am greatly indebted to Val and Eric Grieve, Craig Morrison, Morag and John Wilson, Andrew Pearson, and Lynne Roper for their help and observations.

The secret of staying young is to have fun, laugh often, eat slowly, be friendly, travel often... and lie about your age!

ANON.

Introduction

Since 'The Bus Pass Girls', Barbara and Molly, met up, and opted to use their bus passes more regularly, they have now experienced the fun of bus travel by exploring parts of Scotland they had never dreamt of seeing. Wonderful opportunities have been opened up to them, with Scotland now their oyster.

But these are not two innocent wee women. Barbara should not be underestimated as, although she tends to put on airs and graces, there is clearly another side to her. She can still deal with crotchety drivers, snooty passengers and cheeky weans with rapier-sharp patter. Her dizzy mercurial pal, Molly, is a natural at 'gaun her dinger' by using the Glasgow vernacular to great effect, continually demonstrating this with her withering put-downs.

Anybody picking on these apparently helpless older ladies is in for a shock, as their caustic wisecracking tongues can certainly handle all situations. In fact their cheeky brand of irreverent humour is now legendary amongst many of Scotland's coach drivers. But don't get the wrong idea, for they both can be quite helpful and kind when the occasion requires.

And, there may just be some eligible men onboard! Could be fun, eh?

The Official Scotland-Wide Free Bus Travel Scheme for Older and Disabled People

Barbara and Molly are fortunate that the Scotland-wide Bus Travel Concession Scheme, introduced in 2006, is available to them. It provides unlimited free travel on local bus services and scheduled long distance journeys for people of 60 and over, as well as eligible disabled people, who are resident in Scotland.

The aim of the Free Bus Pass scheme is to allow disabled and older (mind you, our two heroines would be most upset if they were referred to as 'old') people improved access to services, facilities and social networks. The idea is also to help promote social inclusion and improve health by advocating a more active lifestyle. In addition it encourages greater use of public transport rather than private cars.

Those eligible are issued with a National Entitlement Card which allows them unlimited free bus travel across the network in Scotland, at any time of day. It is well used because all of Scotland's major towns and cities are served by short and long-distance bus services. The scheme also provides two free return ferry journeys a year to the mainland for card holders living on Orkney, Shetland and the Western Isles.

It is estimated that over 1.3 million cardholders benefit from this Scotland-wide scheme.

Eligibility criteria for free bus transport may, of course, change from time to time.

Meet Bus Pass Barbara

'Some people think I am perjink and have a slight pretension to gentility. Well, to tell you the truth, I do have a distant cousin who lives in Edinburgh's Morningside, and her mother was allegedly a colonel's second cousin twice removed who rode with hounds.

'I live on my own in a small pebble-dash semi in leafy Bearsden, Glasgow. Some people assert that it's the oasis of high mortgages, Mercs, bridge clubs, book clubs, curling, good teeth, and yummie mummies driving four by fours while wearing pastel pants and cute little cardies. They're probably right.

'Sadly, I am a widow, although I suspect that the frightful little man next door has designs on me. Oh, he is so infuriating, I keep having to fend him off. If you ask me he is certifiably delusional. My dear husband, James, who was such a lovely man, retreated most nights to the garden shed to do manly things with his 'Black and Decker', although to be honest he did like a whisky or three, usually consumed in that 'man cave' shed of his as I called it. It resembled a Neanderthal's retreat full of all the other clutter I didn't want in the house, plus bits and bobs for which there will never again be any conceivable need. I don't go near the place now.

'Although, admittedly, I'm not in the first flush of youth, I do try to keep somewhat in shape, though it has to be admitted, when I wear my favourite dress, you know, the one with lots of red flowers, my bosom does look a bit like a floral ski slope.

'I go weekly to see Dorothy, my hairdresser, or

'coiffeur specialist' as I prefer to call her. Got to keep up standards, you understand. Then there's Cilla, my manicurist, who also helps to ensure that I remain presentable, and of course, I would never go anywhere without the lingering fragrance of a dab or two of *Beautiful* about my person. Furthermore it is necessary to keep a watchful eye on one's posture, I always think.

'So, over all, I consider myself to be well dressed, well heeled, and well read. (Well, I do take the *Herald*).

'When I first learned of this free Bus Pass thing, I deliberated. Would someone of my obvious social standing really condescend to use a free pass? After all, I have to think of my position in life. However, the sad reality is that James' half pension, plus my limited savings, means that I have to be prudent in my spending habits. Why should I pay on coaches when there is no need? Anyway, I strongly suspect others of my status take advantage of this scheme, too.

'However, my chief reason for contemplating travelling out and about on the coaches, and I eventually acknowledged this to myself, was that occasionally I feel a teeny wee bit lonely. Coaches have other passengers on them, and with a bit of luck I thought I might just strike up a conversation with a suitable companion, preferably of the same social standing as myself. That was before I met Molly!

'It's funny that we get on so well, but as I have learned she is actually a kind, funny soul. And to be honest I think she was a bit lonely, too.

'James and I lived very quiet lives. We didn't have a family. I eventually felt that doing the *Herald* crossword, then sitting watching old quiz shows each day on the *Challenge* Network, was not ideal. So, I just said to myself, come on, old girl, why not see some of Scotland for free? After all, when James was alive we had an annual holiday in Arran. But apart from that, and a week once in Tenerife, my experience of travel is very limited indeed. Wouldn't it be nice to visit Edinburgh, Oban, and the likes? I haven't been anywhere for yonks.

'My only real concern was the worrying thought that these coaches might be full of, well, 'common' folk, not to put too fine a point on it. It just shows you that one should not to be so elitist. Now my best friend in the world is Molly, and we are having the time of our lives.

And, let me tell you… boy, is she something else, an absolute hoot! She's what they would call nowadays 'off the wall', but such fun to be with.'

Meet Bus Pass Molly

'Naw. Ah don't stay in a posh hoose like ma new frein, Barbara. But some o' the neighburs are okay. Some others are in and oot o' the jile mair often than the cludgie. Well, that's whit happens when ye stay in a cooncil high rise, ah suppose. Mind you, there' nothing like a wee bit o' stairheid gossip.

'Ah'm noo oan ma tod since ma son emigrated, an' ah finally gave that layaboot o' a husband o' mine the heave-ho. Lazy is no' the word fur it. Ah mean, ah had tae take cleaning jobs – polishin' flairs, scrubbin', dustin' and vacuumin' other folks' hooses jist tae make ends meet.

'That pain o' a man did nothing but slouch around the hoose. His socks never matched. Always at half-mast. An' he wore the same auld jumper wi' gravy stains aw o'er it. Just moaned aboot his poor, wheezy chest an' knocked aboot like death oot fur a dauner. An' another thing, he wis aye smellin' o' BO, lager and Vick. They say a Scottish gentleman is somebuddy who hauds the door open fur his wife tae go tae the midden. Aye, well, he wis that kind o' gentleman. He wis workin' class like the rest o' us. The problem wis he didnae work. So, as ah felt the best years o' ma life were flying by, ah finally gave him the push.

'Ye see, ah might no' be the sharpest knife in the box, but wance ah make up ma mind on sumthin', then that's it. So, he had tae go. Definitely had to go. Went tae stay wi' his sister. An' noo ah've heard she's chucked him oot, tae.

'Ah wouldnae say ah have a temper, but ah can occasionally take a flakey an' let fly at somewan who really gets up ma humph. An' another thing, see if ah have a wee drink in me, then it's probably better best tae stay oot ma road. Ah tend tae shoot fae the lip, as they say.

'Ah certainly wisnae gonnae spend the rest o' ma days looking efter that lazy lout? Ma maw wis right. Ah could've done better. Ah needed tae get oot the hoose mair noo he's awa and have a bit o' fun. Life wis passin' me by. Ah never seemed to go anywhere, really. Jist tae the shops, an' the fatty club.

'So, wan day ah opened ma purse, no' that there wis much in it, an' whit did ah see… ma bus pass. Ah use it tae go intae the toon an' roon aboot here an' there, ye know. As ah say, let the bus take the strain. But, ah says tae masel, sure ah could use it aw roon Scotland, sure ah could? As ma auld faither used tae say, 'adventure afore dementia', though ah don't think he had o'er much adventure. So ah jist says tae masel ah'll jist treat yours truly an' go a day here an' there roon Scotland wi this bus pass. Explore the country a wee bit, eh? That's the very thing fur me, says I. An' that's when ah met up wi' Barbara.

'Aw, she's lovely, so she is. Real class.'

CHAPTER ONE

Their Adventures Begin... off to Dunoon

The huge departure board at Buchanan Bus Station in Glasgow flickered hypnotically as it changed with endless places, times and stance details. An intriguing variety of destinations throughout Scotland were continually on offer... all for free to the 'chosen ones': those with free bus passes.

As Barbara Sharp made her way through the busy concourse towards it, she suddenly felt her leg brush against something unyielding. 'Watch ye don't trip,' came a voice, and looking round she saw a woman of around her own age with a mesmerising face and laughter lines defying you not to smile back, looking at her.

'Thanks,' replied Barbara before glancing at the obstacle. It was the leg of the girl in the famous kissing statue, Wincher's Stance, as she bade her boyfriend farewell. 'It's been a while since anybody gave me a kiss like that,' she smiled wistfully.

'Me tae,' replied the friendly lady. 'Lucky lassie tae hae a boy like yon. So, where are ye aff tae the day?'

'I don't know,' Barbara replied uncertainly while plucking at her tan shoulder bag. 'I just thought it

would be good to get myself out of the house. Maybe go
somewhere nice. A change of air, as they always say.'

'Me tae,' came the reply. 'Ah'm Molly, by the way,'
holding out her hand.

'Oh, right, then.' She hesitated before replying, but
shook hands. 'I'm Barbara. Have you been on many
coach trips?'

'Naw, naw. No' really. Jist buses aroon Glesca. This
is ma first time goin' a bit further. A wee adventure
you might say. Listen, if yer on yer oan what say we go
thegither, eh? A bit o' company. God knows ah could
dae wi' it. See ma ex – useless. Waste o' space. An'
quite a number o' the folk ah know keep dyin'. Dead
inconsiderate. Ah'm thinkin' o' getting' a season ticket
fur that crematorium. An' whit ah find is amazin', is that
in they card shops the Get Well cards are always next to
the With Sympathy wans.'

'Yes. Unfortunately I have also lost a few friends who
have stepped off this mortal coil, as they say.'

Barbara sized Molly up. She was wearing trousers,
a glitzy top and a pale blue anorak. Looked like the
typical Glasgow person of a certain age; small, stocky
and with a robust complexion. A bit common, but keen
to be friendly. And she brought to mind the persistent
little robin who followed her around her garden – head
cocked, bright eyed, expectant. Why not? Try it once,
anyway. 'That would be fine,' she replied. 'I'm actually a
widow. My James died two years ago.'

'Sorry tae hear that. But that would be smashin' tae

get a wee bit company. So where dae ye fancy fur oor first trip?'

'First trip? But we may not like it or even get on together, Molly,' replied a most unsure Barbara.

'Dinnae worry, we'll get oan like a hoose oan fire. Ah can tell,' said the enthusiastic Molly. 'Where dae ye fancy? Personally ah fancy Dunoon. Ah know somebuddy that did it recently. An' ye get two free cruises across the Clyde thrown in. Magic, eh?'

'I don't fancy the thrown in bit,' smiled Barbara. 'But that sounds quite nice.'

'Ah remember as a wee girl going doon the watter wi' ma family, an' throwing stones into the Clyde at Dunoon,' reminisced Molly. 'Years ago it wis gie popular wi' holidaymakers. Ye could row wee boats, an' play puttin' an' stuff. Let's find oot when the Dunoon bus leaves, eh?'

Looking up at the destination board Molly excitedly exclaimed. 'Quick, looks like it leaves at 9.58 frae stance 51. Hey, that's in five minutes time. We'd better be smart if we're tae get oan it.'

Sure enough, the large white coach, a number '701 ClydeFlyer', was sitting in stance 51. They could see a number of heads at the windows, and it looked as though the 48 seater bus was already quite busy.

Both ladies quickly got out their purses and removed their bus passes, before climbing the four steps onto the coach. The driver, drumming on the steering wheel, glanced at both and quipped, 'You two young ladies away fur a wee gallivant oan ma bus, then?'

'Aye,' replied Molly. 'Two tae Dunoon, please. Ye see, son, the problem is oor chau-foors are cleanin' the limos the day.'

The driver gave her a longer, wry look. 'Aye, sure,' he answered.

Molly further quipped, 'An' see an' drive carefully. Have the decency tae wait till we sit doon. The last bus ah wis oan in Glesca the driver jist shot aff an' gave me the fright o' ma life. An' another thing, son. Ah hope ye've goat the champagne chillin' fur the cruise o'er tae Dunoon.'

The bemused driver raised his eyebrows. He replied, 'Aye, sure thing, hen.'

'An' another thing, son,' replied Molly. 'Ah'm no' a hen. Ah might be an auld burd but ah huvvnae goat a turkey neck or chicken wings.' The driver looked unconvinced.

'Look,' interrupted Barbara averting trouble, 'the two front seats are free. We'll get a nice view as we go along.'

'Great idea, Barbara,' replied Molly enthusiastically. 'Dae ye want tae sit next tae the window?'

'That would be nice. Thank you,' said Barbara sitting down and making herself comfortable.

Before she sat down Molly had a quick look up the aisle of the coach. It seemed to be mostly older people like themselves. Passengers were either peering at the two latecomers, chatting, or looking intently at their iPhones.

Across from Molly and Barbara were a middle-aged couple reading Scottish tourist guides. Their leisure suits, good teeth and white trainers suggested they could be American.

'Good cumfy seats, eh, Barbara?' said Molly sitting down.

'Yes, very nice. And they're leather, too. And I really like the large windows with curtains you can pull over if the sun gets in your eyes.'

'This is Scotland, Barbara. Ah bet they don't use they curtains o'er much.'

'By the way,' said Barbara. 'My full name is Barbara Sharp, and I prefer Barbara to Babs. What's yours?'

'Well, ah'm Elizabeth Mary McDuff, to give me ma Sunday name. But ah prefer Molly.'

Just as the ladies put on their seat belts, it was time for the coach to inch back out of the stance, as prompted by the shrill whistle of a bus station marshall, before it then moved slowly forwards until it exited the huge bus station. The large coach turned left then right, and went down the hill past Queen Street railway station to George Square, the impressive area overlooked by the grand Victorian building of the Glasgow City Chambers.

'Ah wance went tae a rock concert in George Square,' observed Molly. 'It wis jist rerr. Probably woke up aw they cooncillors sleepin' in the City Chambers. Ye know, that square is full o' statues, like Rabbie Burns an James Watt.'

The coach then drove along busy St Vincent Street, the pavements now busy with early morning shoppers, before it stopped to pick up another few passengers.

'Barbara,' said Molly. 'Ah've goat tae say this is a nice comfortable bus. But yer no' gonnae believe this, when ah wis young ah thought single-deckers were fur people that wurnae married.'

Barbara smiled and nodded, 'Oh, right.'

From there the coach negotiated a turn onto the M8 motorway, then the Kingston Bridge over the River Clyde, going west.

'So, Barbara. Ye lost yer man a couple of years ago, eh. Have you ony family?

'Not any relatives in the Glasgow area. Just a distant cousin in Edinburgh, I'm afraid,' replied Barbara with an apologetic look.

'It's a real pity stuck oan yer tod, sure it is. As ah told ye, ah had this lazy lump fur years. Sat an' picked his feet when he watched the telly. Pathetic. We didnae hae a car but he then did drive me tae scunnerdom an' back, so he did. We only had wan o' a family. Ma son, Eddie. Emigrated tae America a few years back.'

'Oh, right,' said Barbara, not quite sure how to deal with this unexpected intimacy.

'Ah've never been tae America. The truth is, Barbara, ah have hardly seen much o' Scotland. So hopefully wi' ma bus pass ah can put that right. They say travel expands the mind. Ah could dae wi' mine expandin'. Better than yer waistline, eh?'

'I hope to do the same, Molly. Although James and I did have some holidays they were very limited. Do you know, I've never even been to Oban!'

'Join the club. Me, neither. Never been abroad. Ah cannae dae hot. Gie me a washoot summer an' a dreich winter onytime. Well, hopefully we can baith put that right. eh, Barbara?

'We'll see how it goes,' replied Barbara cautiously.

'An' did ye come fae a family that wis weel aff, Barbara?'

'Not really. Let's just say we were comfortable,' replied Barbara cautiously, unused to such direct questions.

'Well, see in oor family, Barbara, we were pretty well always skint. The only person wi' piles in oor hoose wis ma faither,' she laughed. 'A right shaker and mover he wis as ma mither always said. Aye, liked the bevvy and drove for a removal company. Ma poor mither wid boil a bone frae her corset in a pot alang wi an' auld boot, then she would throw away the bone and we'd eat the boot. Jist kiddin, Barbara. But it certainly wisnae ham an' hough we had. Thank heavens fur school dinners or ah would have perished. Mind you they wis everyday the same. Cabbage an' mashed tatties served wi' an ice-cream scoop alang wi' mince. Ah can still smell it tae this very day.'

'So, what do you mostly do with yourself, now?' enquired Barbara politely, feeling a little more at ease with her new found companion.

'Nothing much, really. Ah used tae go tae the dancing at the Lacarno ballroom. Ah wis a bit o' a twinkle toes, but naw noo. The auld knees have gone. Arthritis gaes me gyp. Ah jist go tae ma fatty club every week.'

'Fatty club?' ventured Barbara.

'Aye, ye know, a slimming club. A've been trying their diet fur the past six weeks.'

'And what have you lost?' asked Barbara, conscious of her own weight.

'Let me tell you whit ah have loast. The will tae live. Ah love ma chuck and it's been awfy hard sticking tae their deadly diet sheet.'

'Life is so unfair when it comes to diet,' sympathised Barbara. 'I must admit I am a little challenged in the waist department. Although I am certainly not slim, believe it or not I am quite a light eater.'

'Aye, me tae. As soon as it gets light ah start eatin',' joked Molly.

Their coach continued to speed west along the motorway before turning off on the outskirts of Paisley to pick up a few more passengers. By now the 48 seater bus was virtually full.

'Clearly popular trip this,' observed Barbara.

The coach drove on with Glasgow Airport passing to their right, and soon afterwards they could see the imposing shape of Dumbarton Rock and the shimmering blue of the River Clyde stretching before them, with the Argyll hills brooding behind.

'Look, quick, Molly!' enthused Barbara. 'Can you make out the outline of the Sleeping Warrior on the top of the hills? It looks like a man lying down, eh? I read somewhere that his eye is supposed to be Castle Crag near Ardentinny.'

'Oh, ah see it,' said Molly. 'But is it no' a wee bit naughty wi' his thingummy stickin' up?'

'No, no. That's his nose! You've got it the wrong way round, Molly,' giggled Barbara.

Further along the M8, Port Glasgow came into view, and with it Newark Castle, glowering, somewhat furtively, on the shore of the Clyde.

The American lady leaned over the aisle and drawled. 'It says here in our guide book that this is Newark Castle and it's awfully well preserved, over five hundred years old! It has battlements, turrets, spiral staircases. Just awesome!'

'Aye,' replied Molly. 'But imagine being stupid enough tae build a castle right next tae a motorway, eh?'

All three looked at Molly. Was she serious? Barbara was slowly getting used to her new friend's sense of humour, but did Molly really think…? No, no way, surely?

As they passed through the industrial town of Greenock they ogled at a massive cruise ship berthed at the Ocean Terminal, not far from the main road. It was clear from the number of people walking around with maps and guidebooks that many of its passengers were busy exploring the town centre, while no doubt others were away on trips to various parts of the central belt of Scotland.

'Ah bet ye some o' they passengers are awa tae the Trossachs or Embra on trips,' speculated Molly. 'An' they'll be paying plenty! An' here's us wi' oor free bus passes. Lucky auld us, eh?'

The coach drove on further down the coast road, past impressive stone villas built for merchants in the town's shipbuilding heyday to the popular seaside town of Gourock, where it stopped at its Pierhead, adjacent to the railway terminal.

'Look,' pointed out Barbara. 'There's a small ship just leaving the pier.'

'Aye,' piped up the driver, 'that will be the ferry tae Dunoon. But it doesnae take cars or buses. Just passengers. Naw like the auld days when there would be umpteen steamers and ferries going all over the place. We need to drive a bit further doon the coast to the Western Ferry terminal at McInroy's Point. That's where we'll join one of their roll-on, roll-off ferries to take us over to the other side o' the Clyde.'

The coach followed Gourock's seaside-hugging road, until it joined a queue of traffic in the first lane of the large parking area at McInroy's Point, a promontory sticking out from the coast. A number of vehicles were already waiting to join a ferry. Soon they saw one of the ferry crew signalling for their coach to go down the ramp to board the waiting ferry. As they did so the coach seemed to rise in the air.

'Hey, driver,' asked Molly, 'Whit's the game? Whit's happening tae oor coach?'

'Nae worries,' replied the driver. 'Ye see it's only coaches on this route, no' buses, because wi' coaches we can hydrolically raise up the vehicle so that its bottom doesnae hit part of the ramp as we drive onto the ferry. Some buses would bottom out.'

'Sure that's awfa clever, Barbara. Eh?' said Molly. 'They think o' everythin' nooadays. Mind you, ma bum widnae mind if it got a wee lift up tae! Might help pull up ma orange-peel thighs.'

As the coach edged slowly forward down the ramp onto the car deck of the ferry, *the Sound of Shuna*, Barbara asked the driver, 'Excuse me, but how long does it take to sail to the other side of the Clyde? You see, I'm not a very good sailor.'

'Just twenty minutes, and the watter looks calm the day so you've got nothing to worry about. Anyway, these ferries are aye steady, even in rough weather.'

Once onto the large car deck of the ferry, the coach door was opened, letting in a gust of fresh salty air, and allowing passengers to exit the vehicle if they wished. Seagulls could now be seen wheeling and heard noisily screeching overhead. The driver then proceeded to pull out his *Daily Record* plus a pencil, and started on a crossword.

'Nae champagne, then?' Molly asked the driver.

'Naw, sorry. That's jist fur the first class passengers. You're travelling coach!'

'Wur aw travelling coach, driver.'

'Coach means those that are not up front on a plane,' explained Barbara.

'Ah've never been oan a plane,' said Molly. 'Maybe wan day we'll get a Plane Pass, eh? Never mind, ah'll jist away an' visit the 'ladies' on this ferry,' added Molly. She reached for her large handbag before going down the stairs, and off the coach.

Five minutes later she was back.

'Help ma boab! Look whit a bliddy big seagull dropped on me.' She lifted her handbag to show the 'offering'.

The American lady opposite fished in her bottomless bag and produced some wipes to clean off the mess.

'Thanks awfy much,' said Molly gratefully.

'I hope you are enjoying your time in Scotland?' asked Barbara politely. 'Where do you live in the States?'

'San Diego, California.'

'Oh, that's a coincidence,' piped in Molly. 'That's where ma son, Eddie is. He lives in a condom there.'

The American woman, her husband and Barbara all smiled, resisting a range of tempting replies.

As the ferry chugged its way across the sparkling river, the village of Strone – mostly a mix of Victorian houses and 1970s bungalows, could be seen to their right, sitting at the head of the Holy Loch.

'Oh, the Holy Loch,' smiled Molly excitedly. 'That's where the American sailors were based aff the Polaris submarines years ago. An' let me tell ye, no' many o' them wis holy. Mind you, if ah had played ma cards right ah could o' married wan o' them and be in America the day. Aye, Big Sam frae Boston wis a right stoater, ah can tell ye. Gies me a wee tingle jist tae think o' him. An' he wis clever. No' like the numptie ah married. Ma ex wis a dead ringer for the skinny wan in Laurel an' Hardy films. Couldnae read a book unless it had pop-up pictures. Did you have ony other fellas afore you married yer man, Barbara?'

'Well, yes,' replied Barbara, her eyes suddenly alight. 'One or two. Like you I sometimes wonder how life would have gone if I had married someone else. One especially, Kenneth. Went to Australia and married someone out there, I believe. I still think of him,' she added wistfully.

Soon the *Sound Of Shuna* slowed her progress before nudging her way into the ferry terminal of Hunter's

Quay on the Argyll shore where the coach, along with the other vehicles, slowly disembarked. Once on dry land the coach level was adjusted before it turned west, travelling on the seaside road through the small town of Kirn, before going further along into Dunoon. There the swish of its tyres soon ceased as it pulled up at the bus terminus, just beyond the Victorian pier.

Dunoon is the main town on the Cowal Peninsula, famous for all the steamers which, many years ago, brought thousands of holiday makers 'doon the watter'. Technically it is in the Highlands. It is famous for its Cowal Highland Games, and as one of the towns much favoured by the Royal National Gaelic Mod, a festival celebrating Scottish culture.

The coach slowly emptied of its passengers, many of them clearly quite stiff from sitting so long. Molly and Barbara said goodbye to the American couple and hoped they would enjoy their time in Scotland.

The 'Bus Pass Girls' were last off. 'Thank you, driver,' said Barbara politely. 'It's been a very smooth journey.'

'It's okay, musses. Ah wis goin' this way onyway,' chipped in the driver with a grin.

The duo stood in the sunlight looking around, trying to get their bearings from local landmarks. Behind them was the River Clyde with the Cloch Lighthouse on the far side of the river. A number of container ships, a frigate and some ferries could be seen in the distance. Inland was Dunoon's shopping centre, and a small hill with a large statue beckoned directly ahead of them.

The day remained bright, with only a few clouds looming on the horizon, ideal for strolling on Dunoon's prom or even through the shops.

'Do you know anything aboot Dunoon, Barbara?' asked Molly. 'Ah wis jist a wean the last time ah wis here.'

'Not much. I read that Harry Lauder lived here. And Burns had an affair with a Mary Campbell who came from Dunoon. In fact, I believe that large statue just ahead on that small hill is probably her. She's referred to as 'Highland Mary'. Do you know that song, *Bonnie Mary o' Argyll*?'

'Ah do. We got it at the school. But you'll be pleased to know that ah'm no' gonnae sing it tae you. Burns wis a bit o' a lad, eh? A statue o' a girlfriend here, an' wan o' him in George Square.'

'Yes,' replied Barbara. 'And I believe there are statues of Burns all over the world.'

'Well, Barbara,' asked Molly. 'What do you say to a plate o' soup an' a cup of tea an' a toastie, eh?'

'That would be just lovely. I'm getting a bit peckish. There's a hotel over there to the right which looks inviting. Shall we try it?'

'Aye. Okay. But ah'm no' often in hotels.'

It was just a short stroll to the Argyll Hotel, and soon they were sitting comfortably in its pleasant restaurant enjoying lunch. It was deserted apart from another two women with specs on chains, ash blonde hair and silk blouses, talking in plummy voices about someone called 'Elister'. One was extremely fat and the other extremely thin. They had been passengers on the same coach, but ignored Barbara and Molly. A pained-looking waitress with a white blouse and a below the knee apron over a straight black skirt, stood in the corner ready to take orders.

'So, we're both oan our own,' said Molly. 'Saves ye the trouble o' cleaning up efter a man, eh?'

'Would you have another man if the right one came along?' asked Barbara with a smile.

'Aye, if he wis a 95-year-old coffin-dodger, had jist won the lottery an' didnae smoke. Smokin' gets up ma nose so it does. It wid gie ye the boke. Ma man wis a bit o' a philistine so ah'm no' keen oan another filla steyin' wi' me,' she joked. 'Aw ye dae is change wan person's set o' irritatin' habits fur another's. Mind you, if he had just won the lottery we could be livin' aff the fat o' the land. See me, ah jist kerry it aboot wi' me,' she said, patting her stomach. 'Whit aboot you, Barbara? Fancy another man?'

'I doubt it, though they do say that late-flowering romances can be a bit special. The widower next door is always at me to go out for lunch. I can't stand him. The conceit of that little man with his eye-rolling smiles. He is always showing off about something or other, and polishing his Porsche to within an inch of its life.'

'Ah hate men like that. Ah prefer wans that are self-defecating,' replied Molly. 'Anyways, whit the hell wis he polishin' his porch fur? Bad enough keepin' it painted, ah wid o' thought.'

Barbara could not contain her laughter but covered it up as much as she could by saying, 'Mind you, Molly, the likes of that silver fox, George Clooney, could put his shoes under my bed, anytime.'

Molly looked afresh at her new friend, her tea cup suddenly stopped in mid-air. 'Oh, ah'm gobsmacked. Ah think there's mair tae you than meets the eye, Barbara Sharp,' she grinned. 'But ye know whit they say, never run after a bus or a man, for there will be another wan alang in a minute. An' by the way, I've got to say you are lovely in that cream leather jacket. If George is in Dunoon the day then ye never know yer luck.'

'Thanks.' Barbara appreciatively stroked the buttery hide between her French manicured thumb and forefinger. 'I love sales. There is something addictive about them. A bit of worship at a "temple of retail therapy" does me good. A sales notice in a shop window always lures me in. Actually, I mostly shop at Marks and Spencer. However, they say a bargain is usually something you don't need at a price you can't resist.'

'Aye, they have nice things, Marks. Sometimes ah might buy something oot o' there, tae. But we have a smashin' charity shop jist alang the road frae me. Pick up some stuff noo an' again there. But ah dae prefer Marks fur ma bras. Ah need wans that are sturdily engineered, ye might say, otherwise it's like two pups fightin' under a blanket.'

'Excuse me, Molly,' interrupted Barbara, 'but I just need to take my pills. I usually take one when I eat.'

'Aye, ah'm under the doctor tae wi' aw ma pills.
An' he's nae 'Doctor Kildare'. Ah remember that
Richard Chamberlain. He wis ma pin-up at wan time.
Noo it's Charlie in *Casualty*. See this gettin' aulder
business, eh?'

'Well, it does have some compensations, like the free
bus pass we're using today, Molly.'

'True enough, but wan o' the disadvantages is that
ah've noo got tae the stage where ah've got tae sit doon
tae put oan ma tights.'

'Me, too, if ye want the truth,' replied Barbara with
a smile. 'By the way, I can't help but notice that is quite
a size of a handbag you have with you. It has a pretty
pattern on the side but it looks a bit heavy.'

'Aye, well ye see Barbara, ah thought as ah wis goin'
quite far oan the buses ah wid need some things fur
emergencies.'

'Good idea, but you seem to have
the kitchen sink in there.'

'No' really. Jist things like
ma readin' glasses,
purse, stickin' plaster,
some ladies private
'you know' things,
lipstick, a screwtap,
nail clippers, a
hairbrush, keys,
paracetamol, and a
book tae read in case

ah didnae meet onybuddy tae blether tae. Plus a few bits and pieces including ma mobile, though ah hardly use it.'

'Good grief, you're certainly well prepared for all contingencies, Molly. But why do you have a screwtop opener with you?'

'Ma fether always said a screwtap is handy. Mine is a screwtap and a wee screwdriver combined. Very useful, ah can tell ye.'

'Oh, right. Listen, I see a notice saying there is a museum in Dunoon. Would you mind if we spent a few minutes in it? Could be quite interesting.'

'Naw, naw, ah wid probably quite enjoy that,' said Molly.

Getting to the museum proved to be a bit of an expedition up a daunting slope past the statue of 'Highland Mary'. A bearded man vigourously rubbing at the door handle greeted them. Spookily, the same man reappeared at the ticket office. And again the same magical sprite urged them into a small, narrow cinema.

'If only yer pal George wis here, ah'd let you two sit in the back seat,' muttered Molly.

Crackling sepia images appeared on the screen. Hundreds of jerky, hyperactive Victorians thronging the pier with multiple ferries in the background.

Then it was on to a proud array of Harry Lauder memorabilia, detailing his incredible impact from his beautiful villa in Dunoon to Times Square, New York.

'What's yer favourite oot o' aw his songs then, Barbara?'

'I quite like, "Will Ye Stop Yer Ticklin, Jock?"'

'Ah think you would prefer, "Don't stop yer ticklin, George",' laughed Molly.

'Now, Molly, you are just being naughty. I think it's time to move on. I see that going by the bus timetable there is a three o'clock coach back to Glasgow. Gets you into Buchanan Bus Station at five past five. How does that suit?'

'That's just grand. It will gae us time fur a wee daunner aroon Dunoon. An' ah tell ye whit, ah fancy an ice cream. What dae ye say?'

As, later, they dawdled along the prom to Dunoon's West Bay, ice cream cones in hand, both felt comfortable in the other's company even though they had known each other only a few hours. Then they opted to sit on one of the many benches along the promenade directly facing the river.

The Clyde appeared at ease; calm and flat. A water-colourist's heaven. It truly was a glorious day.

Looking across the shimmering water they could see the ferry from Wemyss Bay busily steaming over to the Isle of Bute, plus a container ship apparently heading for Greenock. A passenger jet was high up in the now almost blue sky, noiselessly flying over Scotland, probably on its way to North America.

For some time both were caught up with the day. Both were silent, lost for the moment as they savoured the beautiful environment.

Too soon Barbara broke the silence. 'I think, Molly, it's time we wandered back to get the coach.'

At the bus stop they soon realised that it was a different set of passengers from those on the journey to Dunoon. A number had sharpened elbows with bus passes to hand, as they jockyed to get on. And the driver had changed, too. He seemed to be arguing with one of the passengers.

'Sounds as though we have a Mister Grumpy for the trip back,' observed Barbara.

This proved to be true when Molly accidently placed her bus pass on the wrong surface and Mister Grumpy exclaimed, 'Naw, naw! Pit it on here, then sit yer weary bum doon oan ma bus.'

'Listen,' replied Molly in a firm voice. 'I may have a weary bum, but you obviously are a bit o' a pain in the erse.' And, so saying, she and Barbara moved up the aisle to find seats.

Just as they were about to sit down a plummy voice was heard, 'You cannot sit on these seats; they are ours.'

Turning round, Molly and Barbara saw it was the larger of the two ladies with the silk blouses and specs on chains they had noticed in the hotel

'Yes, you see,' continued the woman, 'these are the seats we had on the way here.'

Molly immediately exclaimed, 'Aw, haud me back!'

Barbara said quietly, 'Leave this to me, Molly.'
So saying, she smiled sweetly and replied in her best Bearsden accent, 'Certainly, you may have these seats, ladies, provided you ask the occupants of the front seats to move, as they were the ones *we* sat on coming from Glasgow.' And with that both she and Molly sat down.

'Oh, really!' exclaimed the women in unison while glaring at Barbara and Molly, before eventually opting to sit on the seats across the aisle. They then turned and looked at Molly with all the poisonous charm of a snake when they heard her say, 'That pair must think oor heids are buttoned up the back.'

'Don't worry, Molly. I live in Aga-Saga land, so I know how some people think. Anyway, I enjoy a bit of the old verbal handbags from time to time, especially with people like Hinge and Bracket there. In fact I'm going to call the fat one Hinge and the thin one Bracket. They're the type of people who think breeding is important.'

'Ah've goat a neighbour like that,' said Molly. 'She's got sixteen weans!'

It was not long before the coach set off on its journey back to Glasgow. At the Hunter's Quay terminal a number of white vans and cars were waiting to load. Just as their coach was about to move down the ferry ramp, it was abruptly halted to allow an ambulance to drive first onto the ferry, this time *The Sound of Scarba*, in order to be in pole position up front for driving off.

'That must be some poor soul going to hospital,' said Molly. 'Ah don't like hospitals. Ah had tae go tae the "Betty" fur wan o' they mammograms. See if men had mammograms oan their private parts ye wid hear the squeals all o'er Scotland.'

'Where's the "Betty"?' asked a confused Barbara.

'The Queen Elizabeth University Hospital in Glesca, sure.'

As the coach door was once again open on the ferry, Barbara opted to leave and visit the facilities. As she made her way back up the aisle, she suddenly stopped as one of the passengers sitting in the seats directly in front spoke to her.

When she eventually sat back down again she whispered to Molly. 'I now know why our friends across the aisle were keen to sit here. They must have fancied these two guys in front. In fact I think that one is called Alistair! Certainly one of them winked at me.'

They both sneaked a look at the two women across from them, only to again receive piercing stares.

'Ah love it,' said Molly. 'That's pit their gas at a peep, eh?'

The return trip over the Clyde on the *Sound of Scarba* was slightly delayed, as a Nessie-like Trident submarine and her accompanying flotilla made its way up the river to the Clyde nuclear base.

Once safely back at McIlroy's Point Terminal, the coach lost no time in going through Gourock, passing the famous open-air swimming pool with its heated sea water as it did so.

'Do you swim, Molly?' Barbara asked.

'Naw, unfortunately. Never liked goin' in the water. Ah think it wis because, when ah wis a wee lassie, ah shared a bed wi' oor Magret, and she wis a bed-wetter. Mind you, ah always tried tae sleep in the shallow end,' laughed Molly.

Barbara looked intensely at Molly. Was she really serious or was it just her weird sense of humour?

The return journey to Glasgow's Buchanan Bus Station seemed much shorter than the outward journey. In no time at all they were disembarking at the coach stance. 'Hinge and Bracket' were quick to leave, throwing disdainful looks over their Gerry Weber clad shoulders at Molly and Barbara as they left.

When the 'Bus Pass Girls' disembarked from the coach, feet aching, they came across the two men who had been sitting in front of them.

'Hello, girls,' said one of the men, a chap about their own age with silver hair and a twinkle in his eyes.

'Oh, hello again,' said Barbara. 'That was a lovely day out wasn't it?'

'It certainly was,' replied the other fellow, a slightly older man with horn-rimmed glasses smiling owlishly at them, a tweed jacket, fine cord trousers and a bright red tie.

'Aye,' said the first man. 'Pity we didn't see you in Dunoon, otherwise we could have maybe teamed up for lunch.'

'That would have been very nice,' replied Barbara, looking at Molly to determine her reaction, and twirling her pearl bracelet self-consciously.

'Aye, that wid have been smashin',' Molly replied.

'Do you often go for wee jaunts on the buses?' asked the first fellow. 'I'm Archie, and this is my friend, Alistair, by the way.'

'Pleased to meet you,' said Barbara. 'This is Molly and I'm Barbara. Well, it's our first time away on the buses, as you put it, but hopefully we will be doing other trips.' And she again looked at Molly.

'Definitely,' said Molly, pulling in her tummy and eyeing up the lads.

'Well, Archie and I go for regular trips, so we may well see you again, girls. Bye bye for now.'

And with that they left the ladies standing looking at each other, girlishly.

'Whit dae ye think, Barbara? If we see them again wid ye be quite happy tae, sort of, team up?' asked Molly.

'Maybe, perhaps,' replied Barbara. 'They certainly seemed quite decent. Anyway it would be nice if we could have another wee adventure ourselves. What do you say? Tomorrow is Tuesday and I have a hair appointment. How are you fixed for Wednesday?'

'Ah'm definitely oan fur Wednesday. So will ah see ye here at, say 8.30, and we will see whit's available?'

'I'm looking forward to it already,' said Barbara.

'Aye, an' we might get a lumber,' laughed Molly.

'I thought you said you never wanted another man in your life?'

'True. But ye have tae keep yer options open, sure ye do?'

'We'll see,' replied Barbara. 'Eight-thirty on Wednesday, then. Perhaps Edinburgh?'

'Aye, ah fancy that,'

'I'd better go and get my bus home,' said Barbara.

'Me, tae. Ah need tae skedaddle. But ah cannae wait tae Wednesday. See ye at the Winchin' Stance.'

Barbara's Place, 7.20pm

'I thought I would just sit in my lounge on my dainty Laura Ashley sofa as my Earl Grey hits the spot, and reflect on the events of the day. I love my Venetian green walls with the palm frond design and minimalist goblet pleating on the linen curtains.

'Probably have a little smoked salmon with salad later. See how I feel. The thought just fills me with delicious apprehension.

'When I think on Molly, I can't help but smile. Isn't it nice to have a friend who cheers one up? She is *so* funny.

'There is a long way to go in our relationship but, and I have to admit this, I am truly looking forward to our next trip. I do hope Molly feels the same way. What a character!

'Although I am used to being alone, I feel that today has been a turning point. It's sometimes wearingly easy to slump back and let life just happen instead of wringing out every last great enjoyable minute of it. Today it's dawned on me that what I craved was a true friend. I know that Molly is not the friend I might have envisaged, but we seem to have hit it off. In fact I now feel quite euphoric.

'Wasn't it exciting to travel down the Clyde coast, sail over to Argyll, before sitting in the sunshine on the prom in Dunoon? Just heavenly.

'Ha! I have to laugh when I think of these two woman on the coach who obviously fancied Archie and Alister. And what a nice couple of guys. Normally I consider myself the epitome of cool, but some people can really irritate me. Like my 'stalker' next door. In fact I believe I saw his curtains move as I walked up my path tonight. Mind you, I narrowly avoided my other neighbour, Lucinda Smyth, on the other side, too. Nice enough woman, but always gives me 'mwah-mwahs' and 'dah-ling, you look wonderful' statements. Bit of a gossip. 'You know the type: always wears 'an outfit' with matching accessories – never real clothes. Aren't people and their foibles utterly fascinating?

'Now for a small sherry, as one does. Just to celebrate how today went so well. I'm actually on a bit of a high. My lovely Doctor Pilchard, down at the Health Centre, has told me that in extremis, a little alcohol is good for one's overall health. Oh, and I nearly forgot, it's time for the repeat of *The Archers*.

'And I will need to consider carefully what to wear for our trip when we go to the Capital. Not that I've had many excesses in life but my vanity has survived undiminished. I didn't want to say to Molly but I have a healthy suspicion of anything cheap. Sensible clothes of course – not like her next door. Tomorrow is 'hair day', so Edinburgh is in for a treat.'

Molly's Place, 6.45pm

'The lifts oan ma building were oot when ah goat hame, an' ah had tae come up the stairs. Ah'm fair puckled. So ah jist made masell a wee cup o' tea. Ye cannae beat a cuppa.

'Whit aboot yon Barbara, eh? Mair class than the hale o' this building pit thegither.

'But see if that dug next door doesnae stop yappin', ah'll be right in there.

'Lucky fur me Barbara bumped intae that lovely wee statue at the bus station, sure it wis? Fate it wis, ah'm quite sure. Wis ah lucky or wis ah lucky, eh?

'She's awfa nice and kind. Ah'm that fortunate tae buddy up wi' her. Really chuffed. By heavens, it wis a great decision tae gie masell a kick up the backside an' get masell oot o' ma boring routine. Girls need a bit o' fun. Bus passes sure ur smashin'?

'An' it wis nice tae smell sea air the day fur a change. Good fur the lungs, sure it is?

'An' whit aboot the way Barbara dealt wi' they two 'Trendy Wendies' wantin' oor seats oan the coach. Bloomin' cheek o' them. Good job Barbara got in there first otherwise ah wid o' turned the air blue an' showed masel up.

'Ah think ah should wear somethin' nice fur the next trip as ah'm alang wi' Barbara. Maybe they pair o' black troosers ah picked up at the hospice charity shop. They're practically new. Still had the labels oan them.

An' ye never know, we might bump intae they
two nice fellas again. Ye've goat tae dream,
sure ye have.

'A've jist pit oan ma slippers. They're
rerr an' comfy aroon the hoose. Noo
ah'll jist make masell some oven chips
an' a roll oan butter alang wi' a
swally o' red wine. Cannae beat
it. Ah don't like tae drink
o'er much nooadays. Ye
see the last time ah went
oot fur a drink wi' a couple
o' wummin frae the fatty
club, ah came hame at three
o'clock in the mornin' wi' jist wan shoe. Embarrassin',
eh? Ah seem tae go through a lot o' shoes.

'Noo ah'll jist watch a wee bit o' *Corrie* an' then get
tae ma bed.

'See aw that sea air, fair makes ye tired, sure it does?'

Bus Pass Patter!

On the Aberdeen bus, Molly and the coach driver had fallen out. The argument was getting heated.

'Listen, auld yin,' growled the driver. 'Ah'm no' listening' tae you. Ah can tell by yer face that yer jist a common wee wummin.'

'Oh, aye,' countered Molly, her face moving from hot pink, to traffic light red. 'An' ah can tell by your face you've probably been modelling at an embalmers night class fur years!'

＊

On the bus to Stirling, the extremely fat lady who was taking up two seats, moaned continually about how slow the bus was going, much to the annoyance of Barbara.

'Don't worry, my dear,' Barbara said sweetly, 'It will pick up speed when you get off!'

＊

Barbara was having an altercation with the driver on the bus to Dundee. He was the officious type.

'You might think you are superior, but personally I think you're a poor driver.'

'Ah'm most certainly no' a poor driver. Anyway, you don't need a bus. You should be oan yer broomstick.'

'I've left my broomstick at home, my good man, so you just listen to me. You're the type that is so far up yourself that you could give yourself an enema!'

*

The woman behind Molly was annoyingly belting out pop songs. She leaned forward to Molly and said, 'Ye see, when ah've got problems, then ah sing.'

'Let me tell you, dearie,' replied Molly. 'Ye would hae nae chance oan the *X Factor*. Yer voice is worse than yer problems.'

*

The coach on the way to Campbeltown had been travelling at a speed which alarmed quite a few passengers. Once the driver had to swerve to avoid another bus, at which point he used some very naughty words.

At the terminus he observed to passengers as they trooped off. 'You know, folks, you really only start tae swear once ye learn tae drive.'

'Is that so?' said Barbara. 'And when are you going to learn to drive?'

*

CHAPTER TWO

Off to Edinburgh

As usual, the concourse of Buchanan Bus Station was buzzing with travellers. Suitcases and backpacks were predominant as passengers stood to view the destination board, queue up at the information desk, buy a last minute newspaper or a carry out coffee.

Molly and Barbara shuffled along the queue of passengers waiting to join the Edinburgh coach. Most had bus passes at the ready. Just in front of them a young woman nudged her two children along.

It was a miserable day – raining, grey and dreich, so different from their first day together at Dunoon.

On board, Molly was slow to produce her bus pass from her bag.

'Have ye no' goat yer bus pass ready, yet?' queried the coach driver, clearly keen to get going.

'Aye,' replied Molly smiling, 'Edinburgh, please, but ah'm really hopin' it's ma bus pass tae ecstasy.'

The driver, a balding, middle-aged avuncular figure, looked up and said. 'Ah'm sorry, but we urnae goin' there the day. Maybe the morra.'

Molly laughed. 'Might come an' see ye the morra, then.'

Tickets sorted out and seats thankfully procured, Molly turned to Barbara and observed, 'Hey, yer herr's awfa nice. Dae ye get it done every week, then?'

'I do,' replied Barbara, clearly pleased that Molly had made the observation. 'I feel so much better when it's done. Just a wash and blow dry, you know, with a small amount off the front.'

'Ah wid call that a fringe benefit, so ah wid,' grinned Molly. 'Ah huvnae been tae a hairdressers fur a while. The last time ah went tae get ma hair done it wis rainin' when ah came oot the shop. Ended up goin' hame wi' a poly bag o'er ma heid.

'Barbara,' Molly continued. 'Ah've jist noticed that necklace yer wearin' wi' the gold pendant. It's lovely.'

'Thanks. I like it too. You see it helps cover up a small birthmark I have.'

'Oh. An' how lang have ye had it?'

Barbara gave Molly a quizzical look, something that would be repeated a number of times during their many bus excursions. She was relieved when Molly offered her a smile and a wink.

Apart from the two small children, the passengers were mainly of an age to qualify for free bus passes. It wasn't long before they could hear the inevitable, varying ring tones of mobiles, with some people slow to answer resulting in a jingle going on and on, and then the distant odd, one-sided conversation.

'You know,' said Barbara, 'I get the impression that some people are never happy if they are separated from their phones.'

Directly in front of them a young man with luminous

spots was apparently tone deaf and monosyllabic, as he hummed to music coming through an earpiece.

'Ah'm really lookin' forward tae this trip tae Embra,' said Molly. 'Ah always think Embra is so different frae Glesca. It's jist o'er an hour away frae Glesca but it's, well, another country. The last time ah wis there, an' that wis a while ago, it felt, well, different, ye ken. It's as if Embra has a different kind of air, and there always seems a whistling wind. It doesnae rain as much but feels caulder, ah think. Whit dae you think yersel, Barbara?'

'Well, my memories of Edinburgh are that it is always full of tourists from overseas. And of course there are so many interesting places to see in Edinburgh.'

'Yer right. Ah remember years ago, when ah wis a wee lass, ma granny taking me through tae Edinburgh Zoo fur the day. After that, ma memory o' her is that she wis aye in bed, an' only got oot the bed tae go tae funerals, including her ain.'

'That was most kind of your grandmother taking you to the zoo,' said Barbara.

'It wis. The only problem wis that she wore a hearing aid, an' every time it whistled half o' the animals went daft.'

'I don't really fancy going to the zoo today,' said Barbara. 'But, where would you like to go once we're in Edinburgh, Molly?'

'Ah think they've got they bus tours roon the city, jist like they huv in Glesca. Mind you, ah doubt they'll tak oor free bus passes.'

'Probably not. But that's certainly an idea to think about.'

By now the coach was well out of the bus station, and driving on the High Street passed Glasgow's Royal Infirmary, before negotiating a couple of twists and turning east onto the M8, then picking up speed en route to Scotland's capital.

'Ah told ye aboot ma granny takin' me tae the zoo,' said Molly. 'Well, ma grandpaw – her husband – he wis the fittest man anybuddy ever met. Lived till he wis o'er a hunner.'

'My goodness, longevity must run in yer family.'

'Mebbe. He aye said he wis a deckhand on Noah's Ark. But ma granny wis a stoater. Wance told me that if ye kissed a man twenty times then ye goat pregnant. Oan that basis ah shoulda had umpteen weans, an' ah only had the wan,' laughed Molly.

With the incessant rain outside, and an almost full load, quite a number of the coach windows had steamed up. Barbara repeatedly wiped the window beside her, creating a bit of a smudge in the window's condensation.

Suddenly, both ladies became aware that a wide-eyed, small boy had materialised beside them.

The young lad looked admiringly at Barbara and asked, 'Ur you the Queen, musses. Ur ye wavin' tae aw the people we pass?'

'Aye, son,' smiled Molly. 'She's the Queen an' ah'm a princess.'

The boy turned and ran down the coach aisle to tell his mother that the Queen was on board.

A faint 'Aye, right' could be heard from the front of the coach.

As the coach trundled along the sodden motorway, Molly, on the outside seat, became aware of a rather rotund lady who was occupying both seats across the aisle from her. It was difficult to guess her age as the fat on her blurred any definition of bone structure. Her thighs mushroomed over the edges of the seat. The woman's hair was perfectly coiffed, and her pretty doll-like face was made up as though she was going on the stage. The woman was busy telling all and sundry about her recent cruise, how she had bought a gold Rolex on board, and implying that travelling on the coach was, well, really a bit of a comedown. She turned and caught Molly's eye with something of a smirk.

'You see the problem is that with all my cruising and rich living, I have a problem with my weight. Now I feel there's a thin person inside me trying to get out,' she confessed.

Molly had taken an instant dislike to her, and now just couldn't stop herself. 'Ur ye sure it's jist the wan?' she commented. The woman immediately stopped talking, went white, turned her head away, and tried to peer out of her steamed up window.

Barbara turned to Molly and smiled. 'These people annoy me too.'

The weather improved and it seemed no time before signs for the Heart of Scotland service station appeared.

'Used to be called Harthill,' observed Barbara. 'They keep changing names. Soon we'll see Edinburgh Airport and it used to be called Turnhouse, if I remember correctly.'

At Edinburgh's Corstonphine district, there was a large billboard for Edinburgh Zoo.

EMBRA ZOO   MERRIT

'There has been a lot of publicity,' said Barbara, 'about the two pandas they have from China. I believe the female is called Tiantian and the male is Yang Guang. They have been giving Tiantian artificial insemination as they won't mate.'

'Probably it's because they're merrit,' laughed Molly.

Edinburgh Castle could now be seen, impressively dominating the landscape. The most popular visitor attraction in Scotland.

'Molly,' said Barbara. 'I was just thinking about that small boy believing I was the Queen. Well, I've read and seen documentaries on it, but I've never been to see the Royal Yacht *Britannia*. It's moored at Leith. In fact Leith Walk is, I read in the *Herald*, the most densely populated district in the whole of Scotland.

'Well, there's a lot o' dense folk where ah stay, tae,' said Molly. 'But seriously, that's a great idea, Barbara. Ah forgot aw aboot that boat. See how the other half live, eh?'

'Well, we would probably need to pay to board her. Would that be all right with you?'

'Nae bother, Barbara. Ah jist goat ma auld age pension yesterday. Naw, ah really fancy that. A wee bit special, eh?'

'Well, we could make some enquiries when we get to the bus station in Edinburgh.'

En route, both were able to admire many of Edinburgh's famous landmarks, including the Castle, Scott Monument, and, beside it, Princes Street Gardens. Edinburgh looked to be bustling with shoppers augmented by a stream of tourists gazing up at the castle while referring to city maps, and some consequently tripping over their feet.

'I heard,' said Barbara, 'that the Balmoral Hotel beside Waverley Station always keeps its clock three minutes ahead, just so that travellers will not miss their trains. Apparently they change it back to the correct time for Hogmanay then afterwards change it back to be fast. Thoughtful, eh?'

Soon the coach drew into Edinburgh's St Andrews bus station, and the aisle filled with passengers, seemingly anxious to get off.

'I noticed this when we arrived back at Buchanan Bus Station the other day,' observed Barbara. 'Why do people stand up before the coach has come to a standstill? Even with holding on to the back of seats they nearly always stumble one step forward or backwards when the coach finally stops.'

As a result Barbara and Molly sensibly opted to remain in their seats and were the last passengers to descend the steps of the coach.

At the busy Information Bureau in the bus station, they explained that they had just come from Glasgow to a red-faced man with a small pen sticking behind his ear. He explained they could indeed get a bus to Leith to see the Royal Yacht. 'See you Weegies,' he commented with a cheeky grin on his face. 'Can ye no' read timetables? No brains, eh?'

'Nae brains? Ah wid say yer mither probably goat yours plus yer wee pen, oot an Argos catalogue,' replied Molly

As they moved away to get their bus, Molly observed. 'Barbara, ah wouldnae mind comin' back and seein' roon Embra another day, especially the castle. There's obviously plenty tae see. Fairly attracts the visitors. Must be guid fur business in Embra, ah would think.'

'Yes, I would be on for another day here. I agree that the castle certainly attracts people to the capital. It's just a pity Glasgow doesn't have a castle, too,' replied Barbara.

'Well, we dae. Castlemilk!'

It was only a ten minutes journey to the dock in Leith where the Royal Yacht *Britannia* had a permanent berth to the rear of the Ocean Terminal Shopping Centre. The weather was much improved, with the sky now turning blue and just a few clouds. And there lay the Royal Yacht, looking immaculate and festooned with flags.

'Looks nice,' said Molly. 'But ah thought it wid be bigger.'

'Well,' said Barbara. 'I must tell you that in a documentary I saw about the yacht, it was explained that John Browns in Glasgow, who built her, had actually used existing plans for North Sea ferries to design her. At that time she was apparently just referred to as "Hull 691".'

'That's amazin'. Ah must keep that in mind when ah order ma ain boat,' laughed Molly. 'Probably a wee wan fur ma bath.'

'I don't know about you, but I wouldn't mind a coffee before we go on board.' suggested Barbara. 'What do you think?'

'Great. An' ah could do wi' a wee visit tae the 'ladies',' replied Molly.

The coffee was most welcome after their bus trips. The dockside café they were seated in was filled with people who had either just visited *Britannia* or were waiting to board.

'Ah'm really lookin' forward to goin' roon this boat,' said Molly. 'Ah remember goin' oan the *Waverley*, doon the watter, wi' ma mither and fether. Ma fether took me doon tae see the engines. Ah don't think he wis o'er interested in them. Probably jist wanted a bit o' peace frae ma mither, if ye ask me. Huv you been oan many boats?'

'Not really,' replied Barbara as she sipped her skinny latte, 'but of course we did the ferry trips across the Clyde a few days ago. When James and I went to Arran on holiday we took the ferry from Ardrossan to Brodick. The only other time was when we were courting many years ago, and he used to row me around a small lake in Rouken Glen Park in Glasgow.'

'He seems tae have been a good man, yer late husband.'

'Basically he was. I must say I miss him. Not bad around the house too. My mother always had a wee saying: "You should never have an argument with your husband when he's doing the hoovering".'

'Ah like that wan. Yer mither wis a wise wummin. But noo ah think oan it it's pity we didnae see yon two fellas we met on the Dunoon trip, eh? Thought they might have been at Buchanan Bus Station the day.'

'Oh, my, my,' smiled Barbara, looking closely at Molly. 'I can only assume you quite liked them, or at least one of them?'

'Well, aye. Maybes,' replied Molly. 'They wurnae too bad as men go, ye understaud. Ah may be gettin' oan a bit but ah'm still waitin' oan ma bus tae ecstasy,' she laughed. 'That Archie looked quite nice. Mind you, ma mither used tae say, the mair ah see o' men, the mair ah like ma dug – an' ah had ma dug put doon.'

'So you are an expert on the male species, then, Molly?'

'Ah'm certainly no' an expert, otherwise ah widnae hae got married tae the wan ah got. Pity, 'cause ah did huv an awfa nice childhood sweetheart. Ah've had ma moments, but ah'll keep them tae myself. Ah know ah finally gave ma man the punt, but ah feel the young wans nooadays ur too quick tae get divorces. Ye ken whit they say: ye only huv tae mumble a few words in church tae get merit, and mumble a few words in your sleep tae get a divorce.'

'Mmmmm. You're probably right,' Barbara said, bewildered again. 'I did read an article recently that stated finding love in later life can be wonderful but may bring tribulations, especially if there are adult children involved.'

'Well, oor Eddie is in America, so ah cannae see ony problems wi' him.'

'Have you finished your coffee?' intervened Barbara. 'Are you ready to go onto the yacht?'

'Yea. Ah'm lookin' forward tae this. A bit special, eh?'

'I believe the *Britannia* is a bit special. Apparently it has its own Rolls Royce on board.'

'That's amazin',' exclaimed Molly. 'They wid be better aff wi' lifeboats. Remember whit happened tae the *Titanic*.'

'Oh, I'm sure they will have them on board, too. The Rolls would be for when they were visiting countries in the British Commonwealth.'

The 'Bus Pass Girls' picked up multi-language audio guides at the reception area, before making their way to the entry gangway along with a line of visitors.

'Very busy, the day,' said Molly.

'What I hate is people waddling in front of you who suddenly stop to gawp at something,' added Barbara.

With the volume of visitors, they found themselves along with a tour group, who all seemed quite mesmerised with being aboard the luxury vessel.

'Aw, look,' exclaimed Molly. 'This is terrific. It's jist like a floatin' palace. Ah've never been in a palace afore, mind you. Hey, that's funny! Ah don't think they're lookin' efter this yacht o'er well. The Royals widnae be happy. Aw the clocks urnae workin'. That wan oan the Grand Staircase we jist passed isnae goin' roon. Probably needs new batteries, ah bet ye.'

This observation was overheard by a lady standing beside them. 'Excuse me, she said, 'but I couldn't help but overhear what you said. I just heard one of the guides say that all the clocks are frozen in time at one minute past three. It was the last time that your Queen Elizabeth disembarked in 1977.'

'Is the queen not your queen, too?' asked Barbara somewhat sharply.

'No. I am from the Netherlands. We have our own queen.'

'Ah've goat tae say that your English is awfy good,' smiled Molly. 'Probably better than ma ain.'

'Anyway,' said Barbara a little guiltily. 'Enjoy your trip to Scotland.'

It appeared from the loud conversations and accents that many of the visitors were American. A tall tanned man wearing a light coloured anorak and leather open-toed sandals turned to Barbara and said: 'Magical place, Scotland. And this is a fine yacht. It's just a pity that our Meghan Markle didn't get to honeymoon on board like a lot of the royal family did.'

'You are unfortunately correct, sir,' replied Barbara politely. 'Especially as there is a honeymoon suite which Diana and Charles would no doubt have used. I understand that a waxwork of Meghan is now in Madame Tussauds in London. But what I like is that this wonderful yacht has been saved for the nation and celebrated. Incidentally, I believe some of your American Presidents have been on board. I noticed a photograph of Ronald Reagan in one of the lounges.'

'Yeah, it looks as though Ronnie was on board. I just love some of his old movies. I must say, as I am presently talking to Scots, and I hope you don't think me rude, that I find you people quite fascinating. Many of you have milky skin, blue eyes, and a love for whisky and that metal pop stuff.'

'That's an interesting observation,' replied Barbara, uncertain if she should define the average American or keep schtum. Perhaps say nothing, she decided diplomatically...

'An' aw these royal lounges an' bedrooms look smashin',' added Molly, keen to be involved in the conversation. 'Best o' furniture. Ah bet ye the auld Duke didnae pit any o' them thegither frae a flat-pack, or as ma ex used tae call it, suppository furniture.'

'Suppository furniture?'

'Aye, ye pit it up yersell. Ah told ye he wis the pits.'

On the veranda deck a number of the visitors stood around, listening to their audio guides or fiddling with their iPhone camera. Others with impressive large lens cameras could be seen taking group photographs while instructing everyone to say, 'sex'.

Nearby the ship's bell hung invitingly. Molly glanced at Barbara who said, 'Oh, for heaven's sake go for it Molly. I can see you're just dying to pull it.'

Sure enough, soon the bell was pealing out, with Molly standing with a childish smile of pleasure on her face.

'Ah remember at school the bell going tae get us in frae the playground. An' if ye didnae come quick enough you got a sore hand,' she said.

'Yes, I remember those days, too,' replied Barbara.

Just then, away in the distance, they heard the 1pm gun being fired from Edinburgh Castle.

'If you were up close when that thing went off then it wid gae ye a fright,' said Molly.

'You're right,' replied Barbara. 'I believe it's fired everyday apart from a Sunday. By the way, I don't know about you, Molly, but I am famished. All we've had was that coffee at the dockside. How about tea and cake in the *Britannia*'s tearoom?'

'Yea, ah could do wi' something maysel,' replied Molly. 'Imagine having cake jist as the royals used tae dae on this yacht. Ah fair like carrot cake. Maybe they wull hae some.'

Indeed carrot cake was available with the tea. Soon both sat happily savouring the delicacies while people-watching around the very full tearoom.

'Did you notice the yacht moored alongside the *Britannia*, Molly,' asked Barbara. 'It's the royal's ocean racing yacht. It's called *Bloodhound*.'

'Naw, ah missed that,' replied Molly. 'Ah would've noticed the name. That bliddy bloodhound in the flat next tae mine cannae stop barkin. Drivin' me up the wa'.'

Their chat was interrupted by a deep sonorous voice. 'Excuse me, ladies, but all the places are taken, apart from the spare chair at your table. Would you mind if I sat with you to take my coffee?'

The man was thin with a threadbare beard, wearing an old donkey jacket with leather patches and a knitted blue tie. He looked at them both speculatively, head on one side, his glasses glinting.

'Please do,' replied Barbara, politely.

Having made himself comfortable, he enquired, 'Are you tourists, ladies?' The accent was English.

'Well, sort of,' said Barbara. 'We have come from Glasgow, just for the day. I assume you're from south of the border?'

'Well placed. I'm up from London with a documentary TV crew. We're doing a series called *Royal Residences* and were filming at Holyrood Palace this morning. We're now doing a few shoots around the *Britannia*.'

'Oh, that's exciting,' said Barbara. 'And when will the programme be broadcast?'

'Probably in the autumn schedule. I say, would you mind being interviewed? Just a few words on your impressions of this old tub, eh?'

Molly looked at Barbara with a 'what do you think?' glance.

'Why not,' said Barbara, looking at Molly for confirmation. 'By the way, I'm Barbara and this is my friend Molly.'

'Lovely to meet you both. I'm Jeremy. Delighted you can assist. That would be grand. Perhaps once you have finished your snack we could move to the bridge? My people are there at present setting up their equipment. Maybe we could have you holding the wheel and saying a few words? That would be super.'

They found a cameraman and a sound recordist busy with their equipment on the bridge, closely watched by a growing crowd of interested people.

'This is awfy exciting, Barbara,' said Molly. 'Sure it is?'

'Yes, it's good fun.'

Turning to Barbara, Jeremy instructed. 'Now, just hold onto the wheel, and what I would like you to do is to say what you think the queen would think about her yacht if she were here today.'

Barbara drew a deep breath, and in her best Bearsden accent said, 'One is delighted to be back on *Britannia*. My family and I have many happy memories of the times we spent on her. One is singularly impressed by how my dear yacht is being looked after here in Edinburgh.'

'Very good,' said Jeremy. 'I can just hear her Majesty saying that. Thank you for that observation, Barbara. Perfect. Now Molly, it's your turn to hold the wheel. Just say what you think the Queen would say about her yacht.'

'Sure,' said Molly, conscious that all eyes were on her, but seemingly getting into the swing of things. She held onto the wheel tightly, looked ahead, her face serious, and proclaimed imperiously in a loud voice. 'Fur heaven's sake, Phillip, pit aw they bleedin' clocks tae the right time. It's drivin' me batty.'

'Oh. Right. Ehm, thank you Molly,' said Jeremy, somewhat taken aback. 'A most… interesting viewpoint, if I may say so. Thank you, both for your help. Most kind. You may perhaps see yourselves when the programme airs in a few months.'

On the coach back to Glasgow, Barbara and Molly looked at one another and had a sudden fit of the giggles as they thought of their experience on the *Britannia*.

'Dae ye really think we wull be in that programme, Barbara?'

'Probably not, Molly. But it was awfully good fun, wasn't it?

'Sure was. Made the day a wee bit different. Mind

you ah still fancy another wee trip tae Edinburgh. There's an awful lot tae see there.'

'I agree, Molly. Let's think about that possibility for the future. So what's our next adventure to be? Any ideas?'

'You pick, Barbara. Ah'd quite like somewhere near the sea.'

'Okay, what about Oban? That's next to the sea.'

'Sounds good, Barbara. Maybe Friday, eh? Ah need tae go tae ma fatty club the morrow, an' that carrot cake won't have helped.'

'Friday is good with me, Molly.'

'Pity we didnae meet up wi' these two lads we saw at Buchanan Bus Station efter the Dunoon trip. They were really nice,' said Molly wistfully.

'Oh, you naughty girl you, Molly. That's the second time you've mentioned them today,' laughed Barbara. 'You're acting like a teenager.'

'Ah think you fair fancied them, tae, Barbara Sharp. Did ye no'?'

'Well, maybe. Maybe. We'll just have to wait and see what the future holds, but it has certainly put a spark back into my life. Now, we'd better go to the Citylink office at Buchanan Bus Station and find out when the coach for Oban leaves on Friday. If I remember my geography of Scotland correctly, then we will probably go through some pretty interesting places before reaching Oban. Anyway, regardless, I'm sure Friday will be another great day out for us 'Bus Pass Girls'. And you never know who we might meet, Molly, eh?'

Barbara's Place, 8.10pm

'I'm sitting here in my kitchen. It faces south-east and catches the best of any morning sun on offer, though it can be cosy at this time of day, too.

Do you know I have the most wonderful feeling of wellbeing! Before I met Molly life was just bumbling along. Now I never know what will happen. Spontaneity is my new modus operandi. Why, I've even missed a couple of my favourite TV programmes tonight – and I don't care. Molly is the complete opposite of me, but they do say opposites attract, don't they? I confess I find her engagingly cranky way of talking quite refreshing. Heaven knows what Lucinda Smyth next door would say if she met her. But as far as I'm concerned, Molly is now my very special friend.

Edinburgh is great. Always hustle and bustle. You meet people from all over the world. In fact you meet all kinds of social stereotypes there. I think up to now I have been a little bit parochial.

The royal yacht was fascinating. Such a rarefied air of pomp and ceremony. And we even bought some fudge in the small shop onboard. I will have some after supper which tonight is organic chicken sandwiches in wheat-free bread and a few raw carrot sticks.

I cannot believe we will appear in Jeremy's documentary, but it certainly gave an interesting angle to the day's proceedings. Really good fun!'

Molly's Place, 7.45pm

'That wis a rerr wee day oot. Me oan the telly? Wow, that wid be exciting, eh. Ah jist hope that ma ex sees it. Wull show him how things have improved since he left. Tae say ah'm beyond chuffed wid pit it mildly.

'An' the Royal Yacht wis jist somethin'. Imagin' goin' roon the world in that, eh? Ye wid need tae win the lottery or somethin' tae dae that. Must buy masel a ticket.

'When ah think o' aw they lovely bedrooms oan *Britannia* it fair makes me think ah should have this place painted. Maybe new wall paper in the livin' room, eh?

'Ah've noo got tae the stage that all of a sudden ma life feels it has mair purpose. Seein' roon Scotland wi' Barbara fur free… terrific. Mind ye, ah'm no' tellin' everybuddy otherwise aw they buses wid be choc-a-bloc.

'Noo, haud oan a wee minute. Ah'm gonnae chap at that wee wummin next door. Her dug's yappin' aw the time an' it's daein' ma heid in. Ah don't really like dugs. Cannae hear *Corrie* fur the racket it's makin'.

'Went next door tae complain aboot the dug, an' she invited me in fur a cup a tea. Actually quite a nice wee wummin. Ah usually cannae stand dugs but this wan wis quite friendly. Tellin' me she lost her man recently. Real shame. Ah didnae lose ma man… ah jist telt him tae get loast!

'Next Barbara an' me ur aff tae Oban. Never been. But ah know it's where ye get ferries tae the islands. Don't think we'll huv time tae dae that, mind ye.

'Ah'm actually dead excited aboot goin' tae Oban. Cannae wait, as they say.'

Bus Pass Patter!

The cheeky wee boy and his mother sat on the seat across from Barbara and Molly on the coach to Dundee. Molly got out her bag of sweets and offered them both one.

'So, what would you like to do when you grow up, son?'

'Ah want to be a bus driver.'

'Well, let me tell ye son, yer maw shouldnae staun in yer way.'

＊

The woman opposite Barbara and Molly was annoying them with her superior attitude.

'Ye can always tell how posh a person is by the stop they get off at,' observed the lady to Barbara.

'So you'll be getting off at Gorbals Cross, then?' responded Barbara.

＊

The bus back to Glasgow from Aberdeen was virtually full when Barbara and Molly boarded. Molly found a seat, but Barbara could only see one where a large man had 'manspread' himself over two seats. Barbara gave him a prod.

Looking up, he growled. 'An' who dae ye think you are?'

'I'm the woman you're mother warned you about. Move over.'

He moved over.

❋

As they boarded the coach to Dundee the driver made a face at Molly. They had crossed swords before. Molly, being Molly, duly made a face back at him.

'Listen, you,' said the driver. 'Ma mither said that if ah made a face at folks and the wind changed, then it would stay that way.'

'Aye,' responded Molly, 'an' by the look o' it yer mither wis right!'.

❋

'Excuse, me,' said the rather staid lady sitting behind Barbara and Molly. 'I notice this bus has two doors, one at the back and one at the front. Which door is it best to get off at?'

'Any wan, dearie. Baith ends o' the bus stop at the same time,' replied Molly.

❋

'The coach was en route to Edinburgh. The American tourist sitting beside Molly drawled, 'Say, does this bus stop at the Balmoral Hotel?'

'Ah hope naw,' replied Molly. 'We're jist pensioners.'

❋

CHAPTER THREE

Off to Oban

The coach to Oban was to leave Glasgow at exactly 8.30am. Although the journey would take around three hours, the route would take them past the likes of Loch Lomond, and over the famous 'Rest and be Thankful' then through Invereray before reaching their destination. It was sure to be an interesting sightseeing day out. In the event it was to prove to be more than that.

For a start the coach driver had seemed in a foul mood. As both ladies waited to hand over their bus passes, they heard the driver continually moaning to the boarding passengers as he operated his ticket machine. Traffic congestion, mindless introduction of one-way systems, the weather, and anything else he could think of was commented on.

Barbara heard him expressing all this continual dissatisfaction, and when it came her turn, she said, 'Oban, please.' Then added, 'Did you get out of the wrong side of the bed this morning, driver?'

The driver looked up at Barbara and Molly, 'Listen, see the roads nooadays, ye've goat trucks wheezin' alang the outside lane wi' only enough power tae crawl past, breakdoons an' roadworks all o'er the place. Drive ye batty. Ye've nae idea. An' another thing, half o' the folk oan this coach the day will be moanin' pensioners, half wull be tourists, an' half wull be folks goin' tae their work.'

'Well, all I can say, driver,' said Barbara, 'is that I hope you're driving is better your maths.'

'Aye, well let me tell you you're lucky tae get on today. We have spare seats. Normally ye have tae book.'

Next it was Molly, bus pass in hand. 'So are you gonnae gae me grief, tae?' the driver asked her.

'No' me, pal,' replied Molly. 'But ah have tae tell ye that ah think this coach probably needs a part replacing.'

'Oh, an' whit's that?'

Molly took her ticket from the machine, looked him straight in the eye and said, 'The nut behind the wheel.' Before moving up the aisle and sitting beside her friend.

'Bit o' a pain, today's driver, eh, Barbara?' said Molly.

'Unfortunately, yes, Molly.'

'So whit did ye dae wi' yersell yesterday, Barbara?'

'Well, as you will be aware it was quite a pleasant day, warm in fact, so I did a little weeding in the back garden. It's not very big, just a small section of grass plus James' old shed; it was his favourite haunt. Then I took the local bus to Waitrose in Milngave and got a few essentials. What about yourself, Molly?'

'Nothin' tae write hame aboot. Went tae the local shops, nearly fell oot wi the wummin next door whose dug is aye barkin, but it turned oot she wis quite nice. Then went tae ma fatty club. Ah jist loast wan pound. Better than nothing, eh?'

'Do you like chocolates, Molly?'

'Aye, ah do. An' ma favourite is they ferocious wans wrapped in gold wi chocolate.'

'Yes. Quite. They are really nice. Perhaps I should go to a slimming class, too, Molly. Might encourage me to lose some weight, though I do find it very difficult. I've tried in the past with little success; very disheartening. I now find that my knees are getting quite sore, especially when I do a bit of gardening. Probably arthritis at my age.'

'Well, tae be honest, ah'm getting oan a wee bit. Ah'm, sixty-nine noo, Barbara,' confided Molly. 'So ah can understaun that. Ah think ah've goat a bit o' arthuritis, tae. See if the lifts urnae workin in oor flats, then goin' up an doon the sterrs can be murder. An' aw ye dae is pass workshy layaboots jist hingin' aboot, an' then gangs o' weans wi scabbie knees an' runny noses. An' see the graffiti, it wid mak yer hair curl. This is the problem wi' getting' oan a bit. As ma mither wid say, when ye get tae a certain age ye need rubbed oot an' drawn in again.'

'Well, perhaps I should tell you my age, too, Molly. Just don't tell anyone else,' Barbara whispered. 'I'm sixty-nine as well. My birthday is on the 11th October.'

'You've goat tae be at the kiddin'! That's ma birthday, tae. Don't tell me we wur born oan the same day. How's that fur an amazin' coincidence, eh? We could be twins,' said a flabergasted Molly, sitting back on her seat to have a good look at Barbara. 'Mind you,' she added, 'Ah think you've worn a bit better than masel. Naw as many wrinkles.'

'No, no, Molly,' replied Barbara. 'You look terrific. If I have a few less wrinkles than you it's only because I'm a little heavier. I must say I detest these women who use Botox. Eventually makes them look like freeze-dried prunes.'

'Och, anyways,' said Molly. 'Ah'm sure we huv a few more years left tae enjoy oorsels. Tae tell you the truth ah wis gonnae send away fur wan o' they funeral plans they are aye advertising oan the telly. Apparently ye can pey them up. But noo ah'll no bother. Oor wee gallivants huv given me a new lease o' life. Ah'll even need tae buy long-life milk.'

'That's nice of you to say so, Molly. I must say I am enjoying our little adventures as well.'

A sudden lurch of the coach made them look out of the window and realise that with all their chatting, they hadn't realised they were now almost at Anniesland Cross, en route for Clydebank, Dumbarton and Loch Lomond.

'I was looking Loch Lomond up on Google,' said Barbara, 'and it says that it's Britain's largest inland waterway.'

'Oh, ah didnae know ye had a computer, Barbara. That's great. Ah've jist goat a wee mobile but wi' nane o' they fancy app things oan it. Ah don't have a computer but ah might treat masell. Ah'm still in the dark ages, ah think.'

'Well, I'm no expert. I don't exactly surf the net, as they say, but if you did get a computer then I could come and help you.'

Molly's face fell. 'Tae be honest, Barbara, ah don't think ye wid be o'er impressed wi' ma place.'

'Molly,' said Barbara firmly. 'That would not influence me. What I am impressed with is *you*.'

'Aw, that's awa nice o' ye saying that,' replied Molly, taken aback and with the sudden hint of a tear appearing in her eyes. 'Thanks very much.'

'And another thing about Loch Lomond,' said Barbara, keen that Molly was not further embarrassed, 'is that a lot of people, especially from Glasgow, keep boats there.'

'It seems all oor travels so far have involved boats, eh?' replied Molly.

'Well, Loch Lomond is one of the largest lochs. I think only Loch Ness is deeper and has more water in it.'

'That wull be so that Nessie can huv her lair way doon oan the bottom,' observed Molly, warming to the subject.

'Could be. You never know, Molly. Anyway, keeps the Scottish Tourist Board in business.'

'Oh, an' ah just love that wee song, 'Ah'll tak the High Road , an' you'll tak the low road. You know, that wan aboot the Bonnie Banks o' Loch Lomond.'

'Yes, it's one of my favourites, too,' replied Barbara. 'And do you remember the old Scottish TV soap, *Take the High Road*? Well, it was apparently mostly filmed in Luss, on the side of Loch Lomond.'

'Ah'm fairly looking forward tae seein' the Loch noo.'

The weather was good, and both ladies could feel the warmth of the sunshine streaming through the coach windows. Soon the vehicle was speeding past the cut-off to Clydebank, before stopping at Barloan Toll at Dumbarton; then stopping once more to pick up passengers on a layby at the Balloch Roundabout.

Here, a tiny youth with his hair shaved into the wood, rings in his ears and nose, and weird tattoos on his arms, who was smelling suspiciously of drink, came aboard. He sat diagonally across from Barbara and Molly.

After getting settled into his seat, he turned around to Barbara and Molly and observed. A mischevious grin spreading across his cheeky face. 'Hey, you two auld yins, dae ye fancy a wee dance up an' doon the bus wi' me? Then ye could maybe invite me back tae yer place, eh? Whit aboot it?'

'Listen, son,' quipped Barbara, 'if you came back to my place all I would do is stick you on the mantelpiece as an ornament.'

A loud cuss was his only response, and he looked away. Soon to fall asleep.

Barbara said, 'I think he has a drink in him. And I have got to say that wherever he comes from, I just hope they've stopped their breeding programme.'

The coach had now picked up some speed as it approached Loch Lomond's Duck Bay. The Loch could be seen in between the trees on the shoreline, and on the far side of the loch Ben Lomond rose majestically, the outline of snow on its summit.

Further on at Luss Village the coach stopped to let off some passengers. 'I remember *Take the High Road* well,' pronounced Barbara. 'Some lovely little storylines.'

'Ah'm sorry, but ah never watched it,' said Molly. 'Too busy watchin' *Corrie*.'

Their route then took them past Inverbeg Hotel and Tarbet, before the coach turned west to the village of Arrocher at Loch Long, where it again stopped.

'Look, Molly, see that mountain ahead, that's Ben Arthur, better known as The Cobbler,' explained Barbara. 'The weather is quite clear today, so you can see the rocky summit. It looks a bit like a cobbler working on his last.'

'Oh,' replied Molly. 'Ma faither had wan o' them fur mendin' oor shoes. Ah don't think he wis very good. Sometimes the wee tacky nails wid stick up and hurt the soles o' yer feet when ah wis walkin' tae the school.'

'That must have been quite painful,' commiserated Barbara.

By now the coach had driven round the head of Loch Long and was starting up the long gradient that is the 'Rest and be Thankful'. Looking ahead at the unforgiving slope, Barbara observed, 'This road is well named. Imagine long ago when people had to walk or go by horseback from place to place, they must have had to stop and rest quite frequently to get their breath back.'

'Aye, it must huve been hard goin' in the auld days. Mind you, me climbing up the stairs tae ma flat on the sixteenth flair when the lifts are oan the blink is nae fun, either.'

Suddenly the coach came to an abrupt stop. It quickly became apparent that two men had waved at the driver to urgently let them on. When they boarded it was obvious that they were walkers, going by their haversacks and walking poles. As they came up the coach aisle one of them seemed to be limping, really quite badly. They stowed their backpacks and poles on the luggage rack, and wearily sat down in the seats directly behind Barbara and Molly. One of the men was slim, fit looking with brown hair turning gray. The other looked an outdoors type; sturdy and with a slim neck. He was shorter than his companion with unruly hair, fair going grey, and with a short beard.

Barbara and Molly could hear them chatting away about how lucky they had been that the driver had stopped to pick them up, and how the one with the limp really needed to strap up his ankle.

Then they heard a clear voice from behind. 'Excuse us, ladies. But would you by any chance have a bandage with you. My friend here has a problem with his ankle.'

Barbara looked at Molly, who shook her head. 'Jist a stickin' plaster.'

Barbara replied, 'Sorry, we don't have such a thing. I wonder, would a scarf be of any use?'

'Yes. That might just do it,' replied the fellow with the limp. 'That would be most kind of you.'

Barbara rummaged in her bag and recovered a scarf, before passing it through to the lads.

'Really kind of you,' said the other chap. 'Perhaps I should explain. My friend Arthur here, I'm Ben by the way, and I have started hillwalking now we've retired. We thought it would be a good idea to climb Ben Arthur as it ties in with our names. Bit silly really, I suppose. It's also called The Cobbler, by the way.'

'Oh, yes,' interrupted Barbara. 'We were just discussing that a little while ago.'

'Well, you see we climbed from the Arrocher side,' continued Ben. 'Got to the top and had our sandwiches. Then we watched some other climbers going through what is called the 'Eye of the Needle'. It's a large rock at the top of the mountain with a hole in it, whereby you can scramble though, then stand on the top of it... but there's a sheer drop below. We didn't risk it. However we foolishly opted to descend onto the 'Rest and be Thankful' side rather than go back down to Arrocher. It was extremely steep and Arthur here lost his footing, and has unfortunately ended up with a painful ankle. Don't think he has totally twisted it otherwise he wouldn't be able to walk.'

'Thanks for the scarf,' interrupted Arthur. 'I have tied it tightly round my ankle and it seems to have given it some support. I'm afraid I'm going to have to buy you a new one.'

'No need to do that,' responded Barbara. 'Are you now going on to Oban, like ourselves?'

'No, we are in the George Hotel in Invereray. Go home tomorrow. Will see if the hotel can get us a doctor. It's just a pity we're not going to Oban too, as we could have bought you a meal for your kindness. Perhaps you could give us your address and we will see you get a scarf back. If not this one then a replacement. Add your email address as well, please, if you don't mind.'

'That would be fine,' replied Barbara, once more fishing in her handbag, this time looking for paper and pen.

Barbara passed through to the men a slip of paper with the necessary details.

'By the way', said Barbara. 'This is my friend Molly and I'm Barbara. We're from Glasgow. We have recently been having little jaunts on the buses. Just having a bit of fun and seeing more of Scotland using our free bus passes.'

'Didn't realise you were of that age,' said Ben. 'Well, we live in Perth and needless to say we have our bus passes, too. We thought we could do some hill climbing if it fitted in with the bus timetables.'

'Aye,' cut in Arthur. 'We took early retirement and have decided to make the most of it. *Carpe Diem* – seize the day, as they say. At least we got to the top of Ben Arthur. We had thought on perhaps doing another hill today, but now with my ankle then that's not an option. Of course,' he laughed, 'a couple of whiskies might just help.'

'Arthur is right,' said Ben, 'and he likes his whisky, as do I. You should understand that Arthur is an old batchelor,' and he laughed. 'I am always kidding him on that he is too frightened to get entangled with a woman. As for me, I've only recently untangled myself from one. In other words I just got divorced.'

'Well, we have only become friends in the last week or so,' said Barbara. 'We just met at Buchanan Bus Station, and this is our third away day together. Hopefully we will do many more.'

The girls were sorry when the coach reached Invereray some twenty-five minutes later, and the lads got ready to leave. Barbara and Molly stood to shake hands and say goodbye, but instead got hugs and kisses.

'Listen, girls,' said Ben. 'Why don't you make one of your bus adventures Perth? We could meet up and take you for a meal. And of course return your scarf. What do you say?'

Barbara and Molly looked at one another, and Barbara replied, 'Oh, that would be lovely.' Molly, somewhat reluctantly, nodded her agreement.

'Right,' said Arthur, quickly giving them an old envelope on which he had written his email. 'Just give us a couple of alternative dates and we'll fix something up.' And with that the men collected their gear and exited the coach.

'They wur friendly enough, ah suppose,' observed Molly as the coach once more set off.

'Quite nice lads, I thought,' said Barbara.

'Aye, but ah bet ye they're both merrit. Ah didnae believe aw this bachelor an' divorce stuff. They had oan wedding rings.'

'So how would you compare them to your ex, Molly? Would you have him back?'

'Him! Listen, ah widnae have him back even if he had started tae fart gold bricks.'

The seats vacated by Ben and Arthur were quickly taken by two young noisy lasses who boarded in Invereray. The girls chattered on loudly, mostly about fashion and boys.

'Ah think ah've made a mistake buying these new troosers,' one of the girls was heard to say. 'Whit dae ye think?' she asked her companion.

'Ah don't know. Why don't ye ask they two auld yins in front o' us? They look like fashion experts, ha, ha, ha,' giggled the other girl.

Barbara and Molly gave each other looks at being so described.

The girl on the outside seat suddenly stood up and moved to look at the 'Bus Pass Girls'.

'Hey, youse. Whit dae ye think. Dae they troosers make ma arse look big?' she laughed, giving a little wiggle.

'Naw,' replied Molly. 'If ye ask me, it's too much lager an' chips!'

The young girl gave a snort, looked at them both long and hard before returning to sit behind them.

Then they heard her say. 'Whit dae ye think o' that? They two huv nae fashion sense, whitsoever.'

The coach was now continuing its way towards the Glen Orchy Hotel at Dalmally. However, the stop at the hotel was to prove Barbara and Molly's last bit of the journey on the coach... as the vehicle stubbornly refused to go any further.

After some minutes, when it was obvious that there was a problem, the driver shouted up the aisle. 'Sorry, folks, the engine is going as you can hear but ma gears have packed in. Ah'll need tae phone fur help and a replacement coach. Could take a couple of hours.'

The girls behind Barbara and Molly were heard to say, 'Well, we're certainly no' gonnae push it! Get aff quick afore anybuddy else. We'll thumb a lift.' And they scrambled their way down the passage and off the coach.

'Oh, dear,' said Barbara. 'Well, unfortunately I suppose these things do happen. I think we had better get off, too. At least it is dry.'

Barbara and Molly descended from the vehicle and stood with the other passengers on the grass verge. The two girls were standing in front of the coach, almost in the middle of the road, trying to thumb a lift.

'Oh, for goodness sake! These stupid girls will get

themselves killed,' exclaimed Barbara as a number of cars whizzed by.

Suddenly a police car zoomed past, came to a sudden halt and reversed back. A police officer, a small pert blonde woman, got out, and shouted to the girls to stand at the side of the road, not in the middle of it.

'Good for the police officer,' said Barbara. 'Silly girls.'

The police officer then walked over to the bus and chatted to the driver who was clearly telling her of the predicament. The police officer looked at the group of passengers standing at the edge of the road. Her eyes seemed to light on Barbara and Molly. She came over. 'Where are you going, ladies,' she asked politely.

'Oban, officer,' replied Barbara.

'Right, that's where we're going. Can't take everybody but we'll give you two ladies a lift.'

Barbara hestitated for a moment. The thought immediately flashed through her mind... heavens, what if someone saw her in a police car of all things?

Molly on the other hand was quick to answer. 'Awfy kind o' ye. Mind ye, it wull be the first time ah've been lifted by the polis.'

As they drove off in the police BMW, the two young girls made faces at them. Barbara and Molly merely smiled and waved serenely back.

The police driver, a wiry, fit looking fellow with jutting cheekbones, swivelled round, 'Are you comfortable, ladies?'

'Aye, fine,' replied Molly. Barbara didn't reply. She was too busy keeping her head down to avoid anyone seeing her, though at this juncture the patrol car was merely flashing past fields of sheep.

'We have radioed in,' said the policewoman, 'and told them your coach has broken down. And I'm pretty sure the driver will be arranging alternative transport to take the remaining passengers into Oban.'

Relative to the coach, the BMW smoothly swept along the road, and, in no time at all, the outskirts of Oban came into view. Then it was along to the town front at the harbour where the patrol car came to a halt.

'This is it,' smiled the policewoman. 'Journey's end.' Looking directly at Molly she said, 'Can I tell you a secret, madam? The reason I offered you a lift rather than any other of the passengers is that you look a bit like my old Auntie Jeanie.'

'Aw, right,' replied Molly, clearly stuck for an answer.

'Think nothing of it,' smiled the officer. 'I'll tell my old Auntie Jeanie I met her double today, and, of course, we'll just charge the lift up to the tax payer, eh?'

As the police were about to drive away, leaving the 'Bus Pass Girls' standing on the edge of the pavement, Barbara heard a familiar voice.

'Oh, how lovely to see you, dawl-ing.'

Turning to identify the sound, she was horrified to see her neighbour, Lucinda Smyth, bearing down on her, while at the same time looking closely at the now departing police car.

'Oh, you see, Lucinda,' Barbara blurted out. 'Our coach from Glasgow broke down and the police kindly gave us a lift into Oban.'

'Oh, I truly understand, dawl-ing,' came the non convincing reply. 'How exciting for you. And who is your friend, may I ask?' looking closely at Molly.

Barbara drew a deep breath, mentally saying to herself that she was not going to be intimidated by the likes of snooty Lucinda, a well-known dab hand at causing trouble.

'This,' she said proudly with a smile, 'is my very best friend, Elizabeth. And this, Elizabeth, is Lucinda, a neighbour,'

'Delighted to meet you,' responded Molly, quickly summing up the occasion and putting on a surprisingly elegant voice.

'Oh, delighted to meet you, too,' responded an uncertain Lucinda, still eyeing Molly up and down.

'Yes, Lucinda,' continued Barbara. 'Unfortunately the coach we were travelling on had a technical problem, but a passing police car, with a very charming police officer, kindly offered us a lift. I must get off a letter to the Chief Constable commending his officers. And how long are you in Oban for, Lucinda?' she asked, now steadily recovering herself.

As Lucinda opened her mouth to reply, a man hurried up and directly addressed her, 'Okay, darling, the hotel can take us.'

If looks could have killed the fellow would have

dropped on the spot! Lucinda, her face now a bright red, and with a tiny vein throbbing at the corner of an eye, spluttered to Barbara and Molly, 'Sorry, must go.' And left them standing while she tottered off, followed a few feet behind by the man.

'Interesting,' observed Barbara, a smile spreading across her face. 'Very interesting, indeed. I think that more than cancels out us being in a police squad car. Somehow I don't believe our Lucinda will be spreading any stories around the neighbours about me.'

'Aye,' said Molly. 'She's the type that could be dangerous. We've goat wan or two o' them in oor flats, tae. But ah can sort them oot, nae bother.'

'Right,' said Barbara. 'I think we should treat ourselves to a meal now all the excitement is hopefully over. And perhaps a couple of G&Ts would not be inappropriate. Furthermore, we need to enquire if there will indeed be a coach later on back to the city.'

'Ah hope there is,' replied Molly. 'Otherwise ah wull need tae buy new knickers.'

The 'Bus Pass Girls' stood for a moment surveying the unfamiliar scenery and getting their bearings.

'There is plenty to see and do here,' explained Barbara. 'You can get ferries to most of the Western Isles. And see up there on that hill dominating the town, well, that's apparently called McCaig's Tower, it's a Folly. So it's not totally built. Looks like the Colosseum in Rome. And the Queen's Hotel, that white building ahead, it has two towers on either side that look like the nibs of pens.

Well, it was at one time the home of the famous Parker family who manufactured pens. And the island just out in the bay is Kerrara. You can get a small ferry to it. I always thought Oban would be an interesting place. Pity we are only here for a short time, but we really must first of all check that the bus this evening will run okay.'

They found out that the 6.15pm bus to Glasgow would run as scheduled from bus stance three at Oban Station Road. Reassured, Barbara and Molly had a meal in the Piazza Restaurant as Molly didn't fancy the local speciality of fish.

'Dae ye think that Arthur or Ben wull email you aboot us goin' tae Perth?' asked Molly.

Barbara smiled sweetly while looking at her companion. 'You seem a bit skeptical. Molly. However, as they say, it's all written in the stars. We will just need to wait and see. Now, do you fancy a walk along the front and maybe a wee look at the shops? Then a refreshment, eh? After all the excitement, I think we deserve one.'

'Aye, but as far as ah'm concerned the most important thing on ma mind is this. Ah know your age, you know mine, but just how auld is this auld Auntie Jeanie?'

Barbara's Place, 11.45pm

'With the coach going to Oban breaking down, I was worried in case we would have to spend the night there. But in the end all was well.

'I have never before met anyone born on the same day as myself. It is amazing. I am not really into astrology and that sort of thing, but perhaps it was written in the stars that Molly and I would get together. It is just so nice when I think on it. And assuming we are still friends in October we will be able to exchange birthday cards, and perhaps a little present, too. Lovely thought.

'Poor Molly. This Auntie Jeanie thing has really upset her. I think Molly looks good for her age... just like me.

'That chap Ben was a bit of a flatterer. Said we didn't look old enough to have Bus Passes, the rascal. Of course I do like a man who says nice things, even if they are not always totally true. And Molly seemed happy enough to see the lads, I think, though she suspects they may be married. We'll see.

'Molly and I have agreed some suitable days to go to Perth, so I will wait until tomorrow then send off an email to Arthur. The men won't be home until then, anyway, and I don't want to seem too keen, you understand.

'And what about that Lucinda Smyth? Wasn't it just brilliant when that chap came and foolishly told her, right in front of us, that he had managed to get a hotel for the night. You just couldn't make it up, could you? And she is the one who always seems to regard herself as the epitome of cool. If it got out it would be the talk of the steamie, as they say, though we don't have such a thing in Bearsden. So I doubt if I will be seeing our Lucinda, the curtain-twitcher, for some time.

'Yes, all in all, I feel that things have definitely taken a turn for the better now that Molly and I have started our liitle jaunts. To be honest she is now more real to me than anybody else I can think of. Suddenly all seems right with the world.

'Oh, and I forgot to say that both of us slept most of the way back to Glasgow. To tell the truth we had more than one little drinkie-poo. It was so refreshing to just "rest one's eyes" after such a long day.'

Molly's Place, 11.30pm

'Sure that wis a rerr day oot tae Oban. Quite a distance, but it wis worth it.

'Although we had a drink in Oban, ah jist had a wee swally o' wine when ah came hame. Well, it's supposed tae be good fur yer heart, an' it wis relaxin' efter such a long day oot, is whit ah say.

'Amazin' the coach breakin' doon. Ah bet that disnae happen o'er much. An' the polis comin' an' takin' us intae Oban. Wow. Ah couldnae believe it. Ah've seen plenty o' folks roon here gettin' a ride in a squad car, but it's usually oan their way tae the polis station. Poor Barbara, she wis black affronted, especially when that smug neighbour o' hers saw us getting' oot the polis car. Boy, did her attitude change when that boyfriend o' hers arrived. Hell mend her!

'The only thing that has upset me is the polis wummin sayin' ah looked like her auld auntie Jeanie! An' ah cannae also get o'er Barbara an' me sharing the same age. Even tae the day. A wee bit uncanny if ye ask me.

'And whit aboot they two lads we met up wi'? Appeared quite nice, but ah widnae be surprised if they are really merrit. Ah know whit men can be like. We'll jist have tae wait an' see how it aw turns oot, as ma mither always said. An' another thing she said wis, if yer dream is tae be as good as a man then ye lack ambition!

Anyways, Barbara said she would send me a text if she got an email frae that Arthur.

'An' another thing that's annoyed me. See that plant pot ah pit ootside ma door, ah think that her next door's dug has peed oan it. It wid scunner ye, so it wid.'

Bus Pass Patter

'Ye know, Barbara,' observed Molly. 'When ah wis a wee lass ah used tae take the bus tae school.'

'Is that right?'

'Aye,' she giggled. 'But ah couldnae get it in through the classroom door!'

*

'Do you read much, Molly?'

'Aye. Ah like autobiographies o' celebrities. Ah never read fiction books cause they're jist made up.'

*

'Does this bus stop at the River Ness,' the American tourist asked Molly as the coach approached Inverness.

'Ah hope so, dearie. Otherwise there's gonnae be a hellova splash.'

*

'Dae ye think they jeans are a bit big fur me?' asked the middle aged woman sitting beside Molly.

'Well, either they're too big on you or ye've goat thighs like a wish bone at Christmas.'

*

'Do you like museums, Molly?' asked Barbara.

'Well, ah quite like occasionally goin' tae Kelvingrove Art Galleries tae look at the pictures. But see that Mona Lisa, as far as ah'm concerned she's nae oil paintin'!'

＊

CHAPTER FOUR

Off to Perth

The 'Bus Pass Girls' delayed their next trip for three days, as Arthur and Ben had eventually communicated they would probably be free for lunch in Perth on the following Thursday.

They therefore opted to get the 9.50am coach from Buchanan Bus Station, later than their usual departing times, as the trip to Perth would only take around an hour and forty minutes. This coach would also stop at Stirling, Dunblane and Gleneagles before reaching Perth.

So, in view of this meeting up with the lads, they decided to get together earlier, have a coffee and a little chat. They met up in the John Lewis cafeteria in Glasgow, directly across from Buchanan Bus Station.

Immediately it was noticeable that both had taken extra care with their appearance. Barbara was wearing her favourite floral dress with the red flowers, and Molly had on a navy shirtwaister dress with a white cardigan.

'Ah'm a bit nervous meetin' up wi' they two guys,' confessed Molly. 'Feels as if ah'm goin' oan a date, an' ah huvnae been oan wan fur a long time.'

'Now, don't be silly, Molly,' replied Barbara looking at Molly closely as she slowly stirred her green tea. 'This is just a nice lunch with two men who want to thank us for helping them when Arther hurt his ankle. Nothing more, I'm sure. So you shouldn't be apprehensive.'

'If ye say so, Barbara, but ah canny help it.'

'Now, let's be honest, Molly. You did take a wee notion for that Ben, I thought, eh?' said Barbara with a smile.

'Aye, well. But ah still feel that pair might be merrit.'

'Mmm. Hope not. I thought your ideal man was ninety-five and had won the lottery?'

'Aye, maybes. But a wid prefer wan aboot thirty-five, wi' high cheek bones, a slight stubble, clear blue intelligent honest eyes, an' thick broon hair.'

'In your dreams, Molly! Look, we are having fun and little adventures on our travels. It's great, and this is just another one.'

'Have ye seen or heard frae that Lucinda, yer neighbour, since we goat back frae Oban?'

'Has not been seen around, thank heavens. Probably still in Oban with her fancy man. The only neighbour I've seen is that pest on the other side who continually seems to be out looking for me. Rushes to help carry in my groceries. Silly little man.'

'Well, at least it's nice to know ye have an admirer, Barbara. Ah havnae goat wan. Anyways, ah don't want another man. Ah widnae hae wan even if ah found him in a lucky bag.'

'Right then, Molly. I think it's probably time we wandered over to the bus station. Make sure we get on okay. Don't want to miss it, do we?'

The Citylink coach was already in its stance with a small group ready to either pay or use their bus passes. A number of student types were also putting their haversacks in the boot at the side of the coach.

This time the driver was a cheery fellow, although he did observe that at least all his passengers today seemed to be British, not like that noisy French lot yesterday who only wanted to pay in Euros.

After boarding, the 'Bus Pass Girls' slowly made their way up the coach aisle looking for two seats together.

'Sit here, ladies,' a voice rang out. They looked and recognised the two men they had met at the end of their Dunoon trip, Alistair and Archie.

'Heavens,' muttered Molly, 'It's rainin' men the day.'

'Lovely to see you both again. By the way the seats behind us are still vacant.'

'Yes, it's nice to see you again, too,' replied Barbara. 'The weather looks warm and settled, something like the Dunoon day.'

After sitting and making themselves comfortable, one of the men, Alistair, turned and asked. 'So, girls, are you off to Stirling, Dunblane, Gleneagles, or as far as Perth like ourselves?'

'Perth. It's a long time since I was in Perth, and similarly with Molly, so we are looking forward to it.'

'And have you been on any other coach trips since we last saw you?' asked his friend, Archie.

'Well, after Dunoon we did Edinburgh and Oban. Most enjoyable. What about yourselves?'

'Well, funnily enough we did the Oban run, too. Quite a long journey, but the scenery was magnificent, as you will know.'

The coach had yet to push back from its stance, and a few passengers were still coming onboard. Out of the corner of her eye Barbara saw two women, both wearing tartan jackets, coming up the aisle towards them, their loud plummy voices vaguely familiar.

'Look, Molly,' she whispered quickly, giving Molly a slight nudge. 'Here are our 'friends', "Hinge and Bracket", coming.'

Looking up, Molly exclaimed. 'Aw naw. Ye couldnae make it up. Today looks like a get-the-gither frae oor Dunoon trip. Ah'm no' too sure who Hinge and Bracket were, but tae me they two look mair like Fran and Anna.'

Hinge and Bracket smiled with whitened teeth when they saw Alistair and Archie, their smiles quickly dissipating when they spied Barbara and Molly directly behind them.

'They probably think we are on a day out with these guys,' observed Barbara.

'Serve them right,' giggled Molly. 'Their faces wur fair trippin' them.'

The coach finally started, soon reversing out of its stance, and then leaving the bus station. Alistair turned round to Barbara and Molly and whispered, 'I believe those two ladies who have just come on were also on the coach to Dunoon. I remember they talked to us.'

'Yes,' replied Barbara with a slight grin and a sharp raising of her eyebrows. 'We certainly remember them, too.'

'So have you decided where you are going to go in Perth, today?' asked Archie.

'Well,' replied Barbara, somewhat hesitantly. 'We are actually meeting up with friends for lunch. What about yourselves?'

'We tend to go for museums and art galleries. There is a very nice one on George Street in Perth. Quite interesting exhibits in there, I believe.'

'We were in a museum in Dunoon,' piped up Molly, anxious not to be left out of the conversation. 'Awfa interestin' it wis.'

'Oh. We didn't know there was one in Dunoon. Pity, otherwise we could have visited it.'

It was only a few minutes until the coach maneuvered its way onto a very busy M80 towards Stirling and Kincardine Bridge. Then on past the turnoff for Cumbernauld heading north. By now most people on board were either looking out of the windows, reading a newspaper or chatting, though a few seemed lost in their tablet.

'I have a feeling this is going to be another interesting day, Molly,' observed Barbara.

'Aye. We always seem tae hae a wee bit o' fun everytime we go places, sure we dae?'

It wasn't too long until Stirling Castle could be seen in the distance on the right hand side of the coach, its impressive outer defences sitting atop a crag. Nearby, the famous Wallace Monument was also visible.

The coach duly stopped at Stirling Bus Station, and a couple of passengers got on.

'A lot of history around here,' commented Barbara. 'Perhaps we could visit Stirling Castle one day?'

'Aye, but ah still fancy seein' Edinburgh Castle, tae.'

'Well, I do know that Mary Queen of Scots was crowned at Stirling Castle.'

'Sure she got her heid chopped aff, isn't that right?'

'Unfortunately that is true.'

'Aye, well see if ma neighbour doesnae stop her dog barkin' ah'm goannae lose the heid, cups o' tea or nae cups o' tea.'

The next stop for the coach was the picturesque town of Dunblane just some 20 minutes further on.

Archie, in front of them turned round and said, 'You will know this is where Andy Murray comes from?'

'Yes,' replied Barbara. 'Isn't it great how well he has done. I just love Wimbledon fortnight when Andy is playing.'

'Ah think he's lovely, tae,' added Molly. 'Nice wee bum oan him.'

Then it was on to the next stop, on the A9 at Gleneagles, just opposite the railway station and near the famous hotel. And it was here that Barbara's prediction of another 'interesting day' came about.

Two passengers got off and stood while the driver popped the bus boot and helped them recover their cases. It was as the driver was then getting ready to set off once more and the door was closed, that a loud banging could suddenly be heard on the left hand side of the vehicle. All the passengers on that side quickly peered out the windows. To their amazement, there was a woman, dressed as a bride, red in the face and clearly upset and tearful, knocking to get onto the coach.

The driver immediately opened the door, and the distressed woman came rushing up the steps, almost tripping on her long white train. Flinging herself into an empty seat near the front, she put her head in her hands and sobbed loudly.

'Poor girl,' sympathised Barbara 'We had better go and see what the problem is, though I think I could probably guess.'

The driver, all thoughts of collecting a fare gone, closed the door and switched off the engine.

Molly planked herself down beside the young girl, and Barbara sat on an empty seat behind her. Molly put an arm around the girl's shoulder and said, 'Right petal, tell yer Auntie Molly here whit the problem is? Did he naw turn up at the weddin'?'

Through sniffs, sobs and tears, the girl explained that the morning wedding in Gleneagles Hotel was going fine, until the cleric asked if anyone knew of any reason why the pair could not be lawfully married. Then, a woman at the back shouted out that she was carrying his child.

'Well, I couldn't believe it! I was shocked. Numb. I just screamed and ran out of the hotel. Couldn't think except I wanted to get away from him, the rotten swine. Just ran and ran and ended up here at the main road, and then I saw this coach. He is an absolute liar and a cheat, and to think I thought I loved him. My father spent an absolute fortune on the whole thing. I never want to see or hear from Rupert again!' And at that she again sobbed loudly.

'Aye, men are like that, pet. Ye cannae be up tae them,' consoled Molly. 'Anyway, whit's yer name?'

'It's Caroline,' she sniffed.

'Well, don't you worry, Caroline,' intervened Barbara. 'My friend and I will stay with you until this is all over. Have you any thoughts on where you want to go now?' asked Barbara, trying to be practical about the whole affair.

'I don't know,' sobbed Caroline. 'This whole thing is a nightmare. My brain is scrambled.'

It was at this very moment that everyone on board became aware of a car flashing past, its horn blaring continually. The vehicle tucked itself in in front of the bus, its driver making frantic hand signals.

A young man dressed in black tie and tails appeared outside the coach signalling to the driver to let him in.

Caroline looked up and saw him, then screamed, 'Don't let him in, I hate him and his fancy woman!'

'Sorry, miss,' apologised the driver, 'but we need to resolve this quickly. I have to keep to my schedule.'

The door hissed open and the young man dashed up the steps. He saw Caroline sitting with Molly and Barbara, but before he could say anything Caroline shouted, 'Go away, Rupert. You've ruined my whole life!'

'Darling,' he pleaded. 'I almost caught up with you just before you got on this coach. That dreadful woman is not pregnant with my child. She's lying. I doubt if she's even pregnant. She was a girlfriend about five years ago, and was clearly out for revenge because I terminated the relationship.'

He looked appealingly at Caroline, then went down on one knee in the aisle. 'Darling, I love you more than anyone else. You are my only love. Please believe me. Come back to the hotel and be my wife. Please, please say yes.'

The bride's demeanour radically changed. The sobbing stopped. A smile replaced the upset face. 'Oh, Rupert,' she sighed, 'I do love you, too. Yes, of course I will marry you.'

At this, loud applause broke out thoughout the coach, apart from a clearly heard 'tut-tut,' from Hinge and Bracket.

Rupert smiled with relief and the young couple stood and embraced. Then the bride turned to Molly and Barbara. 'Thank you for your kindness. Why don't you come with us to the wedding as our special guests? My father would be delighted, I'm sure.'

Barbara and Molly looked at one another. For a moment they were clearly tempted. 'Unfortunately,' replied Barbara, 'a couple of friends are meeting us in Perth, and anyway we're not really dressed for a wedding, otherwise we would have been delighted to take you up on your very kind offer, Caroline.'

A relieved groom gave both ladies a kiss on the cheek, the bride hugged them, and the now happy couple departed with a final wave and shouts of 'good luck' from the passengers.

'Well,' said Barbara, as they settled back into their original seats, 'Follow that, as they say.'

'Aw, ah hope it works oot fine fur them. Imagine that wummin kiddin' oan she wis pregnant.'

'Yes, disgraceful. I feel an overwhelming urge to strangle her for putting that poor girl through such trauma.'

'Pity we missed oot oan that weddin' at Gleneagles Hotel. Wid have been lovely, eh? An' that Rupert seems such a lovely guy. A bit tasty. As they say.'

'Yes, they'll make a fine couple.'

The men in front of them turned and said, 'That was very good of you going to help that poor girl. It must have been a dreadful experience for her.'

Molly then thought it opportune to ask, 'Can you remember your weddings then, lads?'

Barbara gave her a quizzical look as she asked the question.

'Well,' replied Alistair, 'I can remember mine, but sadly I am now a widower. And I think Archie won't disagree with me when I say he tries to forget his, as he divorced her a couple of years later. I was his best man by the way. Are you two ladies hitched?'

'Naw,' laughed Molly. 'We're both single, noo.'

'Our lucky day, then,' laughed Archie.

The coach was now making good progress towards Perth, the driver wanting to make up some time. The 'Bus Pass Girls' sat back admiring the rugged beauty and dramatic landscapes of Perthshire flashing past.

'You know,' said Barbara, 'I always think of Perthshire being sublime. And Perth itself is quite an

amazing place. Did you know, Molly, that the River
Tay is the longest river in Scotland and it flows through
the city. And Perth is steeped in history, too. All the
Scottish kings, including ones like Robert
the Bruce, were crowned nearby at Scone
Palace. Anyway, it looks as though we
will soon be in the fair city of Perth, well
just outside it, at the Park and Ride at
Broxden. That's where Arthur said in his
email they would meet us.'

'Whit time does this coach get in, then, Barbara?'
asked Molly.

'Eleven twenty-two according to the timetable.
We may be a few minutes late due to the hold up at
Gleneagles. Oh, I do hope that everything goes alright
for the rest of that wedding. Poor girl. What a thing to
happen on your wedding day.'

'Och, it's a shame. An' they two are clearly besotted
wi' wan another.'

The coach pulled into the Park and Ride beside
Broxden Roundabout on the Glasgow road. It was
running ten minutes late. Barbara and Molly were keen
not to be last off as Arthur and Ben would have had to
wait a little longer than expected.

As they were getting off, they said thanks to the
driver for being so thoughtful with Caroline and Rupert
at Gleneagles. Coming behind them were Archie and
Alistair who, once they were on the pavement, said, 'It
was nice meeting up with you again, girls. No doubt we

will see each other on our travels. See you later and have a really nice day with your friends,' and so saying they joined the queue for a Stagecoach shuttle bus into Perth's City Centre.

When Hinge and Bracket got off the coach, they rudely brushed past and also joined the shuttle bus into the city.

Barbara and Molly looked around; there was no immediate sign of their friends in the melee milling around.

Soon the shuttle bus was full and left, leaving the 'Bus Pass Girls' standing alone at the bus stop.

After ten minutes or so they opted to ask an older man who was manning the shuttle bus information point, if he had 'seen two men waiting on the Glasgow coach?'

'Naw, ladies,' he smiled. 'But if ye haud oan for a couple o' hours ma shift wull be finished, and ah could maybe accommodate ye mysel'.'

'Listen, pal,' answered Molly. 'We might be knockin' oan a bit but we're no' that desperate.'

'Aye, well the next bus frae Glasgow wull be in soon. Maybe yer husbands wull be meetin' that one?'

'They are not our husbands,' replied Barbara firmly

The next bus came and went, with no sign of Arthur and Ben.

'So, what do you think, Molly?' asked Barbara, looking most unsure.

'Well, it's as clear as the nose oan ma face, Barbara. We've been stood up. Ah bet ye ah wis right efter aw an' they're merrit!'

Barbara's Place, 5.35pm.

'What a frustrating day. And it started off so well, too. I was really looking forward to seeing Arthur and Ben again, they had seemed such nice and friendly guys. Talk about being let down. I checked my emails when I got home and there was nothing from Arthur, and I'm blowed if I am going to demean myself by sending him one. I had thought there might be an apology of some sort. Absolutely nothing. I'm fizzing!

'Just think. Molly and I were going to have lunch in Perth with Arthur and Ben, and also, and I am pretty sure of this, Archie and Alistair would probably have liked to have lunch also. And the other thing is we refused to go to Caroline and Rupert's wedding at Gleneagles Hotel. If you thought of all these options which came to absolutely nothing one could be driven crazy. Molly is equally unhappy. In fact I heard her saying a few very naughty words under her breath.

'After we were let down by that pair, we finally opted to get the shuttle bus into Perth. To be fair it is a very nice city. I bought myself a scarf as I am unlikely to see that old one again! But the very worst bit of the day was still to come. We went in for lunch to this rather upmarket restaurant, you know the sort, white tablecloths, well spoken waitresses, classy food, if a little pricy. And who were sitting there together having lunch, but Alistair and Archie plus that despicable pair, fat Hinge and thin Bracket. I have never seen such smug expressions. At least the guys gave a wave over to our table, then Alistair eventually came over and asked what happened to the friends we were supposed to be meeting for lunch? I really felt embarrassed. Completely spoiled the meal. If we had seen the four of them when we first entered then we would have left, and gone elsewhere. But It was too late.

'Molly and I have decided to wait until Friday for our next trip. Put this one behind us. I thought Ayr might be interesting, and Molly seems to especially like the seaside.

'I think I will just put on Classic FM for an hour or so. Try to relax.'

Molly's Place, 5.55pm

'I just had a big tumbler o' red wine. Ah feel ah need tae get a wee bit tipsy efter that day oot tae Perth. Drive ye mad it wid. In fact ah'm still angry as ye might gather. See men!

'Poor Barbara. Ah could tell she wis flamin' mad, too, especially when we saw Hinge and Bracket in that restaurant. Ah've never seen Barbara beelin' afore. Nae wunner.

'Ah've never been tae a posh waddin', an' it's no' gonnae happen noo, is it? Ah jist hope that everything goes aw right fur Caroline an' Rupert. Whit a thing tae happen at yer waddin, eh?

'Actually ah'm a wee bit ashamed o' mysel'. On the way back oan the bus tae Glesca, Barbara and me couldnae sit thegether. Ah had tae sit next tae this wummin who wouldnae stop talkin'. Ah'm afraid ah wisnae in the best frame o' mind, as they say, an' eventually ah got fed up wi her natterin' oan. So ah jist said, 'Listen, you talk that much ah get hoarse jist listening tae ye.' She shut up immediately. An' she wis probably quite a nice person, tae.

'It looks like we are aff tae Ayr on Friday. Ah'm really enjoying aw this chumminess wi' Barbara.

'An' ah jist might get a wee paddle yet.'

Bus Pass Patter!

'I don't like the look on your face,' said the large woman to Molly.

'Well, aw ah can say is that you have goat such a sour look yersell, ah bet ye if you put cream oan yer face it wid curdle.'

❋

'See wi' aw the traffic the day, ah'm at my wit's end', said the annoying driver on the Edinburgh bus. 'So ye cannae blame me fur being late.'

'Wit's end! I'm not going to engage in a battle of wits with you, driver,' said Barbara. 'I never attack anyone who is unarmed.'

❋

'Do you really think us women talk more than men?' asked Barbara.

'Well, ah know English is supposed tae be oor mither tongue, but ah can tell ye in oor hoose ma fether seldom got the chance tae use it.'

❋

'What do you think makes the ideal man, Molly?' asked Barbara.

'Well, ma mither always said that a guid man is wan who wull wash up when asked an' dry up when told.'

✳

'So what is your favourite drink, Molly?'
    'The next wan. Jist kiddin, Barbara!'

✳

CHAPTER FIVE

Off to Ayr

The 'Bus Pass Girls' stood waiting for the driver to process their bus passes. Both peered up the bus aisle to determine if a certain two 'ladies' were on board. They couldn't recognise anyone. In fact Stagecoach x77 to Ayr was pretty empty.

'See if that "Hinge an' Bracket" had been on the bus the day, ah wid o' had a word wi' them, tae pit it mildly,' said Molly.

'Better not to lose your dignity, Molly. Just treat that kind of person with contempt. That's what I say.'

'Aye. Yer probably right, Barbara.'

Soon the bus began to fill up. A stream of noisy young women hooting and chortling, holding bottles of water, and wearing t-shirts bearing the slogan, 'I am a virgin from Glasgow', came trooping up the passage. One of them, a slender woman in jeans and trainers wearing a bridal veil over hair lacquered in a profiterole pyramid, dumped herself down opposite Barbara and Molly.

'Heavens,' observed Molly. 'Naw another bride.'

The girl grinned hazily over at them and said, 'This is ma hen party. An' see the wordin' oan this tee shirt. Well, ah've goat tae confess… it's oot o' date!' she laughed. 'An' noo we're aff tae Magaluf fur the weekend.'

'But surely this bus is going to Ayr?' queried Barbara, who was sitting in the aisle seat.

'Aye, but it stops at Prestwick Airport. Fifteen o' us girls ur goin' on a Ryanair flight tae Palma. Ah'm gettin' merrit a week oan Saturday.'

'Congratulations,' replied Barbara politely.

'Oh, thanks. Wid ye like a wee swally o' ma watter?' the bride asked, holding out the bottle.

'No thanks,' replied Barbara. 'But it is kind of you to ask.'

The girl leaned over, giddily conspiratorial she winked and whispered, 'It's no' watter; it's vodka.'

'Oh, right,' said Barbara, a little taken aback.

'Ah coulda told ye that,' said Molly. 'Ah don't know whit they wull aw be like when they get oan that plane.'

The driver started the engine and reversed out of the stance. Above the drone of the engine the hen party could be heard prattling on before suddenly belting out the Cyndi Lauper song, *Girls Just Wanna Have Fun*.

'Going to be pretty noisy until we reach Preswick Airport,' observed Barbara.

It was at about this time, on the smoother surface of the M77 motorway, that a congo line of the girls formed, and made its way singing, totally out of tune and with much laughter, up and down the aisle. The driver shouted for them all to sit down, and that this wasn't *Strictly Come Dancing*. All to no avail. The vodka was clearly having its insidious effect.

'Sure things huv changed o'er the years,' said Molly. 'Ye widnae o' got this kerry oan fifty years ago. Jist the occasional drunk. See if ma granny wis alive the day, she'd be turnin' in her grave.'

'I must confess that I do like *Strictly*,' observed Barbara. 'But this is not exactly Paso Doble standard.'

The dancing finished as the bus drew into the Village of Fenwick on the Stewarton Road.

'I know about this place,' said Barbara. 'Apparently the Fenwick Weavers Society is one of the oldest co-operatives in the world.'

'Aye,' said Molly. 'Ma mither always shopped at the Co-op. Ah think the dividends kept us aw frae starvin'.'

Fifteen minutes later the bus came to a halt at stop number two, outside Prestwick Airport. After much hilarity, the hen party retrieved their belongings from the bus hold, kissed and hugged the driver, then trailed their suitcases along as they weaved their way towards the airport entrance.

'Noo we might get a bit o' peace an' quiet afore we reach Ayr,' said Molly.

But this was not to be. A few passengers were now coming on the bus, most with tanned gleaming faces from their time in sunnier parts. Included in this group were three older men, all wearing huge smiles, straw hats circled with flowers, Hawaiian shirts, shorts, and open-toed sandals. One had a guitar.

'They are probably from the plane that our hen party are going on,' pronounced Barbara, looking closely at the new arrivals as they heaved various clinking bags on the luggage racks before sitting down. 'I think they may well have been imbibing, too.'

The bus had hardly started before the trio decided to entertain everybody with a full throated version of *Viva Espana*.

'Good grief!' exclaimed Barbara. 'We picked a right noisy bus today, didn't we?'

The guitarist then stood swaying in the aisle. 'Any requests frae you laydeez. We'll sing anythin'.' He stopped, furrowed his leathered brow. 'But maybe no' that "Ness 'n' Dorma"!'

'How aboot singin' quietly?' said Molly.

'Aw, pet, that's no' the attitude. We've jist entertained over a hunner folks oan the plane an' noo we're givin' you that pleasure. Dae ye no' even like ma hat wi' aw they flooers, pet?'

'Ah'm no' yer pet, thank heavens. An' if ye ask me ye've probably got flower disease,' commented Molly.

'Flower disease?'

'Aye, ye look like a blooming eejit.'

'Huh!' grunted the guitarist and sat down. He turned to his companions and said, 'That wummin jist doesnae appreciate good music.'

At stance nine at Ayr bus station, the bus emptied. Barbara and Molly were last off. They stood getting their bearings, then set off in search of a restaurant or café for lunch.

As they sat with their oozing toasties and frothy

coffee, Barbara observed, 'That was quite a noisy trip today. Very different from our other jaunts.'

'Yer right. We didnae get much oportunity tae chat fur aw the noise.'

'So true. I was actually going to talk to you about an idea I have. When we were in Buchanan Bus Station I picked up a leaflet for the Citylink Gold Bus.'

'Gold Bus? Never heard o' it.'

'Well, it's a coach that goes from Glasgow to Inverness or Aberdeen. It's a first class service. You get free refreshments onboard and it has luxury seating. The coach only stops at Perth and Aviemore if it's the one for Inverness. That is where I was going to recommend we go. What do you think?'

'Oh, ah fair fancy that. Never been in Inverness. That sounds smashin'.'

'Well, I've got another proposal for you, too. What about staying there overnight? A sort of mini holiday? Don't worry, if you're not keen then it's not a problem.'

'An' where wid we stay, Barbara?'

'In an Airbnb. You can get quite good deals, I understand.'

'Oh, right,' hesitated Molly, looking most unsure.

'Listen, Molly. Just think about the idea. We don't need to be there overnight, because we could go to Inverness and back on the Gold Bus on the same day if you would prefer that.'

'Naw, it's quite a nice idea. It's jist that believe it or no' ah huvnae stayed in a B an' B or a hotel since ma honeymoon. That wis jist fur wan night in Rothesay a million years ago.'

'As I say, just have a think and let me know. There's no hurry.'

'Okay, ah've thought aboot it! Let's go. It wid be a wee holiday, as you say.'

'You're sure?'

'Aye. The mair ah think aboot it the mair ah like the idea. In fact noo ah'm excited at the thought.'

'That's just terrific, Molly. Perhaps when we get back to Glasgow today we could agree a date and book the coach. Now,' continued Barbara. 'When we finish our snack lunch what would you like to do? Go round the shops, perhaps. Or are you still hankering after a paddle in the Clyde?'

'Well, if ye don't mind, ah wid prefer a wee paddle. Maybe a few shops afterwards. Tae tell ye the truth ah deliberately didnae pit oan ma support tights the day so ah could go intae the watter.'

'Right, then. That's two things settled: paddling and going for a wee holiday, as you put it. I saw the sea glinting in the distance, so I know the rough direction to go in.'

The duo walked down Pavilion Road and were soon on Ayr esplanade and looking across to the Isle of Arran. The outline of the mountain of Goat Fell was clearly seen. Further away, on the outer Firth of Forth, Ailsa Craig stood out mythically.

'Did you know, Molly, that they use granite from Ailsa Craig to make curling stones?'

'Naw, ah didnae know that. But ah remember ma granpaw saying that he saw it when he came over frae Belfast. It's also known as Paddy's Milestone, so ah believe.'

The sky had a few clouds hurrying across and the sea looked a little choppy, but a number of families were picknicking on the beach with small children, clearly enjoying themselves as they frolicked in and out of the water.

'Looks as though the tide is in,' observed Barbara. 'So you won't have to walk far. Just don't get splashed by those children.'

Molly removed her shoes, gave them and her large handbag to Barbara, then pulled up her skirt and gingerly dipped her feet in the water.

'Ooo, it's cold,' she said, quickly getting back onto the sand. Then she had another try, and this time remained standing in the water.

'Very relaxin', Barbara. Salt water is supposed tae be good fur yer feet, ye know.'

Suddenly they both became aware of shouting, and, looking around, saw a man running along the beach towards them, yelling for his dog to come out of the sea.

The dog seemed oblivious to its owner's commands, and continued to swim towards some ducks floating further out. It was only when the the ducks took flight that the dog turned around and swam back towards the beach.

The man, now standing near to Barbara and Molly, shouted 'Here, Oscar! Here Oscar!'

Oscar duly came in through the shallows, stopped precisely in front of Molly and vigorously shook himself, soaking her all over.

'Oscar, you stupid dog!' yelled the man.

'Naw, it's it's a stupid owner who cannae control it!' exclaimed Molly, giving the man a look. 'Look, ah'm fair drippin'.'

'Ah'm so sorry, ma dear,' said the man, clearly embarrassed. 'Ur ye local?'

'Naw, we're frae Glesca an' ah have tae go hame oan the bus in this state.'

'Listen,' said the man. 'Ma wife passed away a few months ago. Ah still have all her clothes. You look the same kind o' build. If you and your friend come up to ma house, and it's only about half a mile away, then you can change. Just help yourself to whatever you fancy.'

'Aw, sorry tae hear aboot yer wife,' sympathised Molly, now completely changing her attitude. 'But ah couldnae possibly take her stuff.'

'Well, if you don't, it will soon be going to a charity shop anyway.'

Molly hesitated, and looked closely at the man. Actually seemed rather pleasant. Probably in his sixties, he had thinning grey hair, a nice smile, and wore a red jerkin. In some weird way she felt she had met him before.

'Dae ah know you, by any chance?' she asked cautiously. 'Ye seem awfa familiar.'

'Funnily enough, ah wis jist wondering if aw knew you, tae. Originally ah wis frae Glesca. Whit's yer name?'

'Ma name's Elizabeth McDuff, but ah'm known as Molly.'

'Heaven's above. Noo ah know ye fine. Ah'm Sandy Cairns. We used tae go oot wi' one another when we were aboot sixteen. In fact, sure we wur in the same class at school.'

'Aw, Sandy,' blushed Molly. 'Lovely tae see ye efter aw they years. So when did ye move tae Ayr?'

'Well ye see ah married a wummin frae Ayr, an' ah goat a job doon here driving buses. But noo it's just me an' the dug.'

'Whit a nice dug,' stated Molly. 'Ah love dugs. Ma neighbour's goat a nice wan.'

Out of the corner of her eye Molly saw Barbara smile.

'And this is ma good frein, Barbara.'

'Please tae meet ye, Barbara.'

'Nice to meet you, too, Sandy.'

'Right, dae ye want tae come up tae the hoose, then? Ah can make ye a cuppa. You'll need tae excuse the place but ah'm no' really intae keepin' it o'er tidy.'

Molly looked at Barbara, who grinned and said, 'Of course Molly wants to come, and so do I. It's very thoughtful of you, Sandy.'

'No problem. An' ah'm dying to catch up wi' you, Molly an' find out whit you've been up tae. We kinda lost touch, didn't we?'

Barbara looked over at Molly, who had suddenly gone all coy.

'Aye, ah don't know whit happened.'

'Ye might no' want tae use it but here's Oscar's towel. Ah huvnae dried him yet. It's maybe no' the best, but if ye want tae wipe yer feet and get the sand off ye can use it. Jist haud ontae me fur a wee minute.'

'That's awfa thoughtful o' ye, Sandy.'

Molly used one hand to hold onto Sandy's arm, as she wiped her feet, then slipped her shoes back on.

Oscar was dried, then they set off on the short walk

to Sandy's house, with Molly and Sandy reminiscing about all the people they had known in their childhood. By the time they got to his house – a middle terrace with a small well maintained garden – they were laughing and joking as though they had never been apart.

Barbara fell back a little, discretely marvelling at this revelation – a gentler, more feminine Molly.

Sandy's wife's clothes were in an upstairs wardrobe. Molly was reluctant to try them on, but eventually opted for a frilly blouse and black trousers. Looking around, she saw a silver-framed photo of a cheerful woman on the small table beside the bed and assumed it had been of his late wife. Then at the mirror she gave her hair a deft brush and put on extra lippy, smacking her lips together, pleased with the result.

When Molly came downstairs, Sandy had prepared a pot of tea and some toast, and was busy chatting away to Barbara. Oscar lay snoozing in his basket.

'Ah see you've changed. You look grand,' said Sandy.

'Thanks,' replied Molly. 'Wid ye hae a plastic bag ah could borrow fur my wet clothes?'

'Sure, nae bother. An' ah'll pour ye some tea and gie ye a slice or two o' toast plus home made bramble jelly. Ah also make the bread masell.'

'And it's really lovely,' said Barbara.

'So you're oan yer own now, Molly?'

'Aye, it never really worked oot wi him. But noo ah've goat ma frien Barbara here, an' we've been having rerr wee jaunts roon Scotland.'

'Ah thought aboot daein' that, even though ah drove the buses masell,' mused Sandy, 'but ah'm a bit stuck wi' Oscar here.'

'Aye, ah can see that. But at least ye have a bit o' company. Ah don't even have a budgie.'

The happy reminiscing continued with no thought of time, before Barbara said, 'Well, I don't like being a spoilsport, Molly, but we should possibly be making our way back to the bus station.'

'Right,' said Sandy, 'let me get ma coat and ah wull walk ye up there. Molly, maybe ye could gie me yer address and phone number? Whit dae ye say?'

Molly blushed. 'Sure, Sandy. That wid be nice tae keep in touch.'

At the bus station Sandy gave both ladies a hug, and also gave Molly a tentative kiss.

'Noo, remember an' keep in touch, Molly.'

'Ah will. Lovely tae see ye again, Sandy.'

Sandy waited until the bus drew out of the bus station, waving until the bus was out of sight.

'I figure that was the childhood sweetheart you once mentioned, Molly?'

Molly blushed again. 'Aye. Isn't he nice, eh? We used tae have wee canoodles in oor back close.'

Barbara gave her a long knowing look as the bus set off on its journey back to Glasgow.

At Buchanan Bus Station the 'Bus Pass Girls' duly booked to go on the Gold Bus to Inverness the following Tuesday for their next adventure.

Barbara's Place, 5.45 pm

'Well, talk about rekindling romance. You could see that Molly has still got feelings for that Sandy. Seemed a really decent guy, too.

'It just shows you. You never know what turns up in life, do you?

It was a good day out though it was a noisy bus going down to Ayr. At least on the way back it was quiet and Molly and I had a wee chat. She was busy telling me about her early life and how she and Sandy had been pals all through school.

'I saw that Lucinda Smyth as I came home. She saw me but completely ignored me. That's fine as far as I'm concerned. Just shows you how embarrassed she still is about that 'Oban incident'. Silly woman!

'I'll just have a look at Airbnb places in Inverness on the net, and maybe book one later. We've reserved seats for next Tuesday on the Gold Bus. It was one pound per person but the bus itself is free if you have a concession card. Well, we 'Bus Pass Girls' certainly do!

'I am still quite full from eating Sandy's toast and jam, so I will leave it till later to have something to eat. I will just have a green tea and a sherry at present, then sit and watch the six o'clock news.

'Probably have a wee snooze as well.'

Molly's Place, 5.50 pm

'Ah'm that mad at masell. Ah gaed Sandy ma address an' phone number but didnae get his. Ah know whit ah'm like. Noo ah'll be worryin' in case he never phones.

'Oh, see that Sandy Cairns! Lovely man. Ah remember his mammy called him Alex. Wid o' made a rerr husband. Even makes his ain breed. Ma heid's in a tizzy. Ah've come o'er aw flustered. Noo ah dinny know whit tae be at. An' tae think he drove buses, tae. Maybe if ah had used ma bus pass mair often ah might o' met him afore noo.

'Ah'll jist hae a wee drink. Try an' calm doon. But, see that wan ah married... useless.

'It wis fair entertaining wi' aw they daft lassies goin' on a hen outing. Ah remember aw ma pals and me jist goin' doon tae the pub fur ma hen party. It's aw different noo, sure it is.

'An' ah goat ma paddle. An' whit a paddle it turned oot tae be, eh? Ah'm no' too keen oan dugs, but noo, ah love that Oscar. If he hudnae o' shook himsell all o'ver me ah wid never have met Sandy again. Mind you, ah don't know if anythin' will come o' it. Stupit me no' gettin' his phone number.

'Noo it's this Gold Bus tae Inverness. That sounds a bit posh, sure it does? Then stayin' the night. Maybe get masell a new nightie. By crivens, ma life has certainly changed since ah started usin' ma bus pass mair regularly.

'An' Barbara is jist terrific. She's a rerr organiser, so she is.

'Aw, naw! There's that dug next door yappin' again. But sure ah've decided ah noo love dugs, sure ah have? Better say nothing, then.'

Bus Pass Patter

The couple and their baby were sitting across from
Molly and Barbara on the bus to Edinburgh.

'My, my,' observed Barbara. 'What a lovely child.
He looks just like his father.'

'Ah know,' replied the woman, then whispered,
'It's jist a pity he doesnae look mair like ma husband.'

✳

The coach to Kilmarnock was passed by a lorry loaded
with turf.

'See if ah win the lottery,' stated Molly. 'That's whit
ah'll dae. Send ma grass away tae get cut.'

✳

The little girl was sitting beside her mummy across the
bus aisle from Barbara.

Barbara smiled at her and asked, 'And how old are
you, darling?'

'I'm four,' replied the little girl proudly, 'and it's
mummy's birthday today. She's twenty-five, and do you
know, she can still ride a bike!'

✳

'I quite like to bake occasionally, Molly. And although
I say it myself my sponge cake usually turns out pretty
perfect,' said Barbara

'Wan o' ma neighbours is intae sponge cakes, tae,' replied Molly. 'She comes tae ma door an' sponges aw the ingredients. Next time she does that, ah'm jist goin' tae tell her tae bake aff, or somethin' like that!'

❉

'You know, Molly,' said Barbara. 'All I read in the newspaper is that if you want to succeed at work nowadays you have to be able to multi-task. My husband was quite good at doing various things simultaneously. What about yours?'

'Him! Oh he wis intae multi-tasking aw right. He could screw up several things at the wan time.'

CHAPTER SIX

Off to Inverness

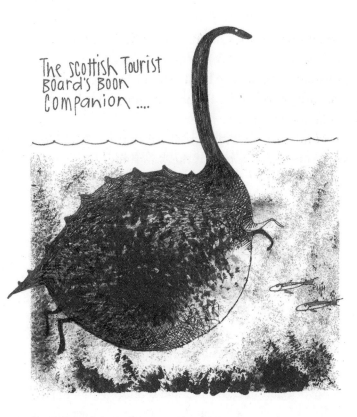

The scottish Tourist
Board's Boon
Companion ....

'Ah, naw!' exclaimed Molly, as they queued bleary-eyed but excited, to join the G10 early morning 7.30am Gold Bus to Perth, Aviemore and Inverness.

'What's the matter, Molly?' asked Barbara, anxiously.

'Can ye no' see who's in the queue ahead o' us? It's that Hinge and Bracket pair. Ah think they follow us aroon.'

'Oh, dear,' said Barbara. 'Well, don't worry, they'll probably just ignore us as before.'

But as luck would have it, when the 'Bus Pass Girls' got onboard they discovered their allocated seats were adjacent to Hinge and Bracket, who slyly glanced at them.

'Listen, Molly. It's a long journey to Inverness. We really can't just ignore them. I think I will try to be friendly. Probably the best thing to do.'

So saying, she turned and said, 'Good morning. We seem to meet up on the same bus trips.'

Hinge looked pained and replied with frosty-eyes in a pan loaf accent, 'We prefer to call them coach trips. Not bus trips.'

'Oh, right,' replied Barbara, unshaken. 'So are you off to Inverness today, like ourselves?'

The smug smiles became even more pronounced.

'No. We are orf to Perth to meet up with our dear friends, Alister and Archie,' she replied with a haughty air. 'I believe you may have seen them in a restaurant with us. Well, it was so successful that we are meeting up there again. The chaps took a coach yesterday as they were attending the races in Perth.'

Barbara gave her a withering look, and turning to Molly whispered, 'What a sanctimonious pair. I should just have ignored them.'

'We were jist unlucky tae be sittin' near them, if you ask me,' replied Molly.

'I did enquire with City Link if it was possible to be seated at the front of the coach. They told me that the seats just inside are for disabled passengers, and you cannot sit in the seats directly behind the driver if you will be wanting a hot drink.'

'How's that?' asked Molly.

'Well, they explained it's in case of emergency braking, and the driver might get hot tea or coffee over him. Listen, Molly. Let's just forget about Hinge and Bracket. Don't want to spoil our mini holiday, do we?'

'Talking aboot men, did ye ever get an email frae that Arthur and Ben?'

'Nothing. And I had thought they were quite nice.'

'Aye, maybe. But not as nice as ma Sandy.'

'Oh, have you heard from him?'

'Em. Not yet,' replied Molly, suddenly looking a little downcast.

'What do you say we forget about men, eh? Did you know that this bus passes Gleneagles, so let's just hope we don't have any more distraught brides.'

'Aye, ah hope that the wedding went aff okay an' that they're noo happily merrit.'

'I'm sure it went fine. They seemed so much in love. Anyway, this bus doesn't stop at Gleneagles. Just Perth and Aviemore before we reach Inverness. We should get into Inverness relatively early so that will give us some time to see the city.'

'Did ye manage tae get us fixed up fur the night?'

'Yes. I spoke to a very nice man at an Airbnb I found on the net. We have single rooms, and it wasn't really expensive. I also picked up a map of Inverness. Did you know it's the capital of the Highlands?'

'Naw, ah didnae. Scotland must have two capitals, then.'

The Gold Coach was well fitted out. Leather seats, excellent WiFi and with plenty of refreshments. Once on the road north, a young lady with a trolley that rattled and squeaked up the the aisle, offered complimentary drinks and snacks. Tea, coffee, water and soft drinks – including Irn Bru in bottles – plus biscuits and tablet were all available.

'This trip is a real bargain,' commented Molly. 'Aw the visitors frae abroad must be really impressed.'

'I'm sure they are,' replied Barbara, 'especially when they look out of the windows at our lovely Scottish scenery.'

Barbara and Molly both chose coffee plus some biscuits. Barbara said to the refreshments girl, 'I notice that the coach is full today.'

'Well, madam, some people will be leaving us at Perth and we will be picking up passengers there off the Edinburgh bus. Then we go on to Aviemore and Inverness.'

'Oh, I see. Thank you,' replied Barbara. 'You are doing a great job, if I may say so.'

'Oh, thank you, madam,' beamed the trolley girl. 'My granny says I am really a bit young to be doing this job, but I like it.'

'Lucky granny to have you,' said an impressed Barbara.

'You know, Molly,' said Barbara once the trolley had moved on. 'I hesitate to say it, but I was just thinking. Compared to our other trips this is all going very smoothly. We can just sit back, relax and enjoy the day.'

The words were hardly out of Barbara's mouth when a scream was heard followed by a loud unmistakable voice bawling, 'I cannot get out. This door is locked. Help! Help!'

It transpired that Hinge had gone to the onboard toilet and become locked in.

A naughty smile spread across Molly's face. 'I read somewhere that toilets on buses could only be used for number ones, but ah bet ye oor friend is doin' more than that right noo.'

'Molly! You are incorrigible,' laughed Barbara.

The trolley girl could now be seen trying to open the toilet door. She was clearly having difficulties. In the meantime the desperate screams of Hinge intensified.

The trolley girl made her way to the front of the coach and was obviously discussing the crisis with the driver. Back she came and had another try at opening the toilet door. All to no avail.

'I must admit,' said Barbara, 'that I feel a bit of schadenfreude coming on.'

'Dae ye take pills fur it?' asked a concerned Molly.

'No, no Molly. The word means enjoying the discomfort of others. It's German. Their polysyllabic words express every dark nuance of emotion in a way no English word attempts.'

'Heavens. You should be oan *Mastermind* wi' aw they big words, Barbara. Well, ah've goat the meanin' noo, tae, ah think,' smiled Molly.

Suddenly Bracket, now red of face, demanded to all and sundry in a loud voice, 'Tell the driver to stop this coach! My friend is locked in. He *must* know how to open that door.'

'Well, he's puzzled as well,' replied the trolley girl trying to calm her down. 'You see we are a wee bit behind our schedule to meet up with the Edinburgh bus at Perth.'

'I warn you, we will get our lawyer onto this. Sue this company. You will all be fired,' shouted an irate, now purple, Bracket.

Then another voice was heard. 'Aw, fur heaven's sake. Let me have a go.' It was Molly, who had fished in her large handbag and produced her screwtop, before making her way to the toilet where sobbing could now be heard.

Molly examined the door, then expertly squeezed the screwdriver part of her screwtop between the slight gap in the door and the location of the lock. She applied upward pressure for a few moments. Suddenly the door swung back to reveal a distraught, tearful Hinge.

'Oh, thank heavens,' cried Hinge, wrapping her arms around a surprised Molly.

'Nae, problem,' was all Molly could manage to reply, before helping Hinge back to her seat

'Thank you so much. I was really worried I would be locked in for a long while. I'm a bit claustrophobic, you see.'

'Well, jist you sit there an' relax, dearie. The trolley lassie wull no doubt get ye a wee drink.'

'That was quite something, Molly,' said an impressed Barbara as her friend sat back down.

'Believe me, Barbara, that wis a doddle. Ah've opened a few cludgie doors in ma time,' grinned Molly.

After the trolley girl had got both Hinge and Bracket drinks, she appeared beside Molly. 'Thank you for helping that lady out, madam,' she said. 'I was getting really worried. May I get you ladies some more refreshments? By the way my name is Dolly,' she confided.

'That wid be fine. Ah'll have an Irn Bru,' said Molly. 'So, you're Dolly the trolley girl. Well, ah'm Molly. Maybe ah could get a job as a trolley girl, too?' and she winked at Dolly.

'I'm fine at present,' said Barbara. 'Perhaps have something later on in the journey.'

The driver announced over the coach tannoy that the toilet would be out of commission for the rest of the journey. However facilities were available at the stops at Perth and Aviemore.

Molly became conscious of a light nervous touch on her arm. 'Excuse me,' said Hinge leaning over the aisle in a soft voice and with an embarrassed smile. She held out out a packet of sweets. 'Would you care to have one?'

'That wid be kind o' ye,' replied Molly graciously. 'An' maybe wan fur ma frien here, eh?'

'Of course. And I am extremely grateful to you for your ingenuity. I must confess I am still shaking.'

Barbara whispered to Molly. 'By golly, *she* has fairly changed her tune. A bit of a lesson to both she and Bracket, if you ask me.'

Molly then replied to Hinge, 'Och, ye'll be okay wance ye've had a glass or two in Perth, eh?

'Well, I don't normally imbibe strong drink,' replied Hinge, 'But perhaps a little brandy might help.'

'Just don't get yersell tipsy if yer goin' tae be wi' those playboys. You know whit men can be like, eh?' and she winked at Hinge.

After all the excitement it seemed that time had just flown by, and soon they were once more in the familiar surroundings of Perth's Broxden Park and Ride.

As Hinge and Bracket left the coach, Hinge turned and mouthed a 'thank you', as her companion stood for a few moments, clearly having words with the poor driver.

A dozen or so people got off, and were immediately replaced by a similar number from the Edinburgh bus which had arrived before theirs.

'That was a disappointing day the last time we were in Perth,' voiced Barbara. 'Those guys really let us down.'

'Sure did,' said Molly.

Once the newcomers were settled in onboard, the door sucked closed once more, and they set off for the next stage of the journey to Aviemore.

Some of the newcomers were talking somewhat loudly and it appeared to the 'Bus Pass Girls' that there had been drink taken, as Barbara put it. Their suspicions were found to be correct when they heard Dolly, the trolley girl, exclaiming loudly, 'Behave yourself. I'm only here to give out refreshments, sir.' Both Barbara and Molly strained their heads to hear what the problem was. The rest of the bus had also gone quiet as the man's voice slurred, 'Come on, pet, gie us a wee cheaper. It's ma birthday.'

'I told you to behave yourself,' came the nervous voice of Dolly. 'Would you like a coffee, perhaps?'

'Naw, come here an' gie me a kiss,' came the persistant voice.

Barbara said to Molly. 'This is intolerable. Excuse me, could you let me out, please. I think it's my turn to be the good Samaritan.'

Barbara strode down the bus aisle, chest suddenly out, a determined look on her face.

'Did I hear someone was wanting a wee cheeper for their birthday?' she asked loudly.

'Aye, me, luvvie. But no' frae you.'

'That's a pity for I will happily give you one,' came Barbara's raised voice. 'Just you close your eyes.' The drunk, a man in his forties with jet black hair and leery eyes, who was apparently accompanied by the grinning man sitting next to him, closed his eyes.

'Here comes your wee smacker!' And a loud slap was heard throughout the bus.

'Hey! Ye nearly had ma false teeth oot.'

'Listen, and listen well, you. Dolly here is my granddaughter and if you don't apologise to her I will ensure the police are waiting for this coach at Aviemore.' And Barbara leaned over the man, eyes staring directly at him. 'You are nothing more than a dirty minded little man. And, furthermore, don't luvvie me!'

Holding the side of his face, the man looked up at Dolly and said meekly, 'Aw, very sorry, hen. Nae harm meant. Jist a wee bit o' fun. Ah didnae realise yer granny wis oan the bus.'

Barbara gave him one last withering look, and Dolly a reassuring glance, before marching back to her seat.

'Nae messin' aroon there,' said Molly. 'Good fur you, Barbara.'

'To tell you the truth, Molly, I quite enjoyed that. I have been dying to hit a belligerent man like that all my life. An arrogant pest, something like that neighbour of mine. Now at least he will hopefully think twice in future about preying on young people.'

'Aye,' replied Molly. 'As ma mither used tae say, 'Some men are jist like pigs.'

Dolly appeared at their seats. 'Listen, I am so glad you ladies are with us today. I don't know what I would have done if I had been on my own.'

'I am sure,' replied Barbara, 'that other people would have helped you out.'

Then it was time for the 'Bus Pass Girls' to once more sit back and hopefully relax, as the coach once again took to the A9 for Inverness.

'You know,' said Barbara. 'We will soon be passing Pitlochry. That's somewhere I went for weekends with my husband a number of years ago. The Festival Theatre there is lovely. Do you know it puts on plays and musicals at West End standards.'

'Sound like a nice place,' replied Molly. 'Ah've only been tae the Pavilion and the Kings in Glesca tae the pantomines. Ah always liked that Stanley Baxter.'

'I enjoy a good pantomime, too,' said Barbara. 'Puts one in the Christmas spirit, I always think.'

'Ah don't need tae wait tae Christmas tae get a wee dose o' spirit,' grinned Molly.

'In that case a little drink tonight might be nice,' said Barbara. 'Perhaps we could slip out to a hotel nearby for a refreshment.'

'Ah'm oan fur that,' said Molly enthusiatically.

The bus continued its way past superb countryside. Glens and rivers with the hills and mountains on either side of the bus climbing steadily higher. Both ladies sat continuously looking out of the windows, admiring the ever changing scenery.

'Nae wunner aw they tourists come tae Scotland, eh?' observed Molly. 'In fact ah feel like a tourist the day. Never been this far north afore.'

'Yes,' replied Barbara. 'Scotland really is superb. I think we tend to take it all for granted.'

It didn't seem long until the coach was pulling into Seagate Bus Station in Aviemore. A few passengers left the coach and some came on, most clearly tourists.

'Ah hope wur no' goanny have ony mair shenanigans frae this lot,' said Molly.

As luck would have it the Aviemore contingent were well behaved, and all was calm with no further incidents on the final leg of the journey to Inverness.

The three and a half hours had passed quickly.

At Guild Street Bus Station in Inverness Barbara and Molly disembarked. It was still relatively early, just 11.00am.

'I don't think we will get into our accommodation at this time,' said Barbara, 'so we may as well look round Inverness for a few hours. I must say it does look very nice.'

'It does,' replied Molly. 'But the first thing ah need tae dae is find a toilet. Ah'm burstin'.'

'Yes, that would be a good idea.'

Toileting over, Barbara suggested thay have a walk. 'I know you fancy a castle and Inverness has one, but we've been on the Gold Bus for three and a half hours. I think a bit of exercise would not be inappropriate. Now, according to my map of Inverness they have a suspension bridge over the River Ness, and then you can walk past some small islands that are also called Ness. Might be interesting, eh?'

'That's fine wi' me. Doesnae look as if it will rain, an' a bit o' fresh air wid be good.'

The late morning proved bright, with the sun coming through to warm the day. On the suspension bridge the duo paused to look at the fast flowing River Ness. A branch of a tree with a little bird sitting proudly on it flashed under the bridge, much to the delight of Barbara and Molly. They met and chatted to a number of people also taking a stroll alongside the swirling waters dashing past the small islands.

After almost an hour, they turned around and made their way back into the centre of Inverness.

'Listen, Barbara, would you mind if ah had a wee nosy in wan o' the charity shops up here. Might jist pick something nice.'

'Of course not,' replied Barbara. 'That would be fine with me. And then we could perhaps have some lunch.'

The charity shop chosen proved to be a bit of an Aladdin's cave, and eventually Molly emerged happy with a white top and two pairs of shoes. 'Labels still on!,' she announced, triumphantly.

'I know that bag of yours is big,' said Barbara,'but with these shoes it's going to be quite heavy to carry around.'

'Och, nae problem,' said Molly. 'Ah'm used tae carryin' this bag aroon.'

'Okay. Perhaps we could have something to eat and then go and find our Airbnb.'

The small restaurant they chose looked inviting. Clean, with starched white table cloths and gleaming glassware. They were fortunate to get the only remaining free table.

'Seems a nice place. So, what do you fancy, Molly?' asked Barbara as they sat examining the menu.

'Ah actually fancy some soup. Ah see it's Scotch Broth, ma favourite. That an' a frothy coffee wull dae me fine. Och, an' maybe a wee cake as ah'm oan my holidays.'

'Perhaps I'll just have a wholefood salad with avocado and some green tea,' decided Barbara.

The waiter proved to be an older man, who promptly tripped over Molly's now bulging bag lying beside her chair and fell directly onto their table, almost knocking over the small vase of flowers sitting on it. Righting himself, he politely said, 'Well, sorry about that, ladies. I seem to have fallen for you.'

Molly replied, 'Naw, sorry. It wis really ma fault. Ah shoulda stuck ma bag under ma chair like ma frien Barbara has.'

Molly looked up at the man to see his reaction. He was a neat fellow with a lean and ageless face. Probably in his late sixties, she guessed. He stood gazing intently at Barbara. Then Molly realized that Barbara's face had taken on a puzzled look.

'You must excuse my bad manners,' the man said to Barbara. 'But you look like someone I used to know long ago.'

'I feel the same, somehow,' Barbara stuttered out.

'My name is Kenneth,' said the man, never once taking his bright blue eyes off Barbara.

'You're Kenneth,' she echoed in a strangely quiet voice.

'I knew a Barbara like you before I emigrated to Australia.'

'And I knew a Kenneth like you before he emigrated to Australia.'

'Oh, Barbara,' said Kenneth, suddenly reaching out and holding her hand. 'Is it really you?'

'It's me. Somewhat older, but it's certainly me.'

Kenneth sat down beside Barbara. 'I went out to Oz, but unfortunately things didn't work out. Made a terrible mistake, so I came back. Then someone told me you had gone and got married.'

'Yes, I married James,' Barbara replied in a trembling voice. 'But he has now passed on.'

'When I came back home I came to Inverness instead of Glasgow. Worked in a large multi-national here, then left and opened this place.'

Shaking off her shock, and grasping her impeccable manners determinedly, Barbara returned. 'Sorry, but I'm being very rude here, Kenneth. Let me introduce you to my friend Molly. We're exploring Scotland on the buses.'

'Pleased to meet you, Molly. Well, I am so glad you both came to Inverness. I can hardly believe this. Have you remarried, Barbara?'

'No,' came the answer in a soft voice.

Molly said cheekily. 'Excuse me, the way this conversation is goin' can ah be yer wee flower girl?'

Barbara blushed. 'Don't be so silly, Molly.'

Kenneth smiled, his laughter lines crinkling appealingly. 'Well, who knows.'

Barbara's blush deepened.

Barbara's Place, the Following Night

'We never made that Airbnb. Kenneth cancelled the booking and insisted we spend the night at his house. A lovely apartment in an old manor house, near Strathpeffer.

'Of course, I didn't sleep a wink. No, not for *that* reason! I was so excited. Kenneth and I sat up until two o'clock in the morning catching up. The woman he married in Australia was unfaithful to him, so he came home. Once he had learned I was 'spoken for', as he put it, he went north to Inverness.

'I now realise I have probably always had feelings for Kenneth. The truth is I have certainly thought about him many a time. I get the impression that he has feelings for me, too.

'James never knew anything about Kenneth but, being the nice man he was, I am sure he would not now object.

'I know we had a few little happenings on the bus coming to Inverness, but they are almost forgotten given that I have met up with Kenneth again.

'If Kenneth and I do get together, then you just never know. Molly just might be our flower girl! Certainly Molly will always be my very best friend. And by golly my neighbours, Lucinda and that detestable wee man, will certainly have plenty to talk about!'

Molly's Place, the Following Night

'Aw, wisn't that jist lovely! Barbara meetin' up wi' Kenneth. They should make a film aboot it. Ah'm really pleased fur her but ah'm even mair pleased fur masell! When ah got hame Sandy had left a wee message oan my phone. To tell you the truth ah danced roon the room then had a wee swally o' wine. Even that bleedin' dug next door didnae upset me, fur once.

'Whit a day it wis yesterday. Aw that kerryoan oan the bus wi' Hinge and Bracket. An' noo ah'm a frien o' Hinge's, though in truth ah don't think ah'm her type. Probably never see her an' her expressionless pal again.

'An' there's nae messin aroon wi' Barbara, is there? Fairly stood up fur Dolly the Trolley. Ah jist loved that.

'Ah jist hope it works oot fur Barbara an' Kenneth, an' me an' Sandy, tae.

'We'll just need tae see how it aw goes. Fingers crossed.'

A Week Later at the Wincher's Stance statue in Buchanan Bus Station, Glasgow

'Good morning, Molly.'

'Mornin', Barbara. Ur ye aw set? Ah see ye huv a case wi' ye.'

'Yes, and I see you have a case as well. It's exciting, isn't it? So when does your bus for Ayr leave?'

'Nine o'clock. Ah'm a bit nervous ah must admit. Whit aboot the bus tae Inverness?'

'Same time. In fact we should really be making tracks. Just to make sure we get on.'

'Yer right. Gae me a phone an' let me know how it aw went. Ah always fancied carryin' a train.'

'Naughty, naughty, Molly! Don't worry. I will phone. Hope it goes well with you and Sandy. So, bye, Molly. Oh, and by the way, just one last thing.'

'Whit's that?'

'Got your bus pass?'

Luath Press Limited
committed to publishing well written books worth reading

LUATH PRESS takes its name from Robert Burns, whose little collie Luath (*Gael.,* swift or nimble) tripped up Jean Armour at a wedding and gave him the chance to speak to the woman who was to be his wife and the abiding love of his life.
Burns called one of 'The Twa Dogs' Luath after Cuchullin's hunting dog in Ossian's *Fingal*. Luath Press was established in 1981 in the heart of Burns country, and now resides a few steps up the road from Burns' first lodgings on Edinburgh's Royal Mile.
Luath offers you distinctive writing with a hint of unexpected pleasures.

Most bookshops in the UK, the US, Canada, Australia, New Zealand and parts of Europe either carry our books in stock or can order them for you. To order direct from us, please send a £sterling cheque, postal order, international money order or your credit card details (number, address of cardholder and expiry date) to us at the address below. Please add post and packing as follows: UK – £1.00 per delivery address; over-seas surface mail – £2.50 per delivery address; overseas airmail – £3.50 for the first book to each delivery address, plus £1.00 for each additional book by airmail to the same address. If your order is a gift, we will happily enclose your card or message at no extra charge.

Luath Press Limited
543/2 Castlehill
The Royal Mile
Edinburgh EH1 2ND
Scotland

Telephone: 0131 225 4326 (24 hours)
email: sales@luath.co.uk
Website: www.luath.co.uk